English Syntactic Structures

Other titles of interest

AARTS, Flor and Jan Aarts
English Syntactic Structures Workbook

DUFF, Alan
The Third Language

FISIAK, Jacek (ed)
Contrastive Linguistics and the Language Teacher

JACKSON, Howard
Analyzing English

LOVEDAY, Leo
The Sociolinguistics of Learning and Using a Non-native Language

NEWMARK, Peter
Approaches to Translation

POLDAUF, Ivan
English Word Stress

English Syntactic Structures

Functions and categories in sentence analysis

FLOR AARTS

and

JAN AARTS
University of Nijmegen

ENGLISH LANGUAGE TEACHING

Prentice Hall

New York   London   Toronto   Sydney   Tokyo

and

MARTINUS NIJHOFF

Leyden   Antwerp

First published 1982 by Pergamon Press Ltd
This edition first published 1988 by
Prentice Hall International (UK) Ltd,
66 Wood Lane End, Hemel Hempstead,
Hertfordshire, HP2 4RG
A division of
Simon & Schuster International Group

Printed and bound in Great Britain at
the University Press, Cambridge

Library of Congress Cataloging-in-Publication Data

Aarts, Flor.
English syntactic structures.
Includes Index.
1. English language—Syntax.   I. Aarts, Jan M. G.
II. Title.   III. Series: Language courses.
PE1361.A2 1981   425   81-21107

British Library Cataloguing in Publication Data

Aarts, Flor.
English syntactic structures.
1. English Language—Syntax
I. Title   II. Aarts, Jan
425   PE1361

ISBN 0-13-281478-1
ISBN 90-6890-2202 (Martinus Nijhoff)

2 3 4 5   92 91 90 89

Preface

This book has been written with the needs of two categories of students in mind: first-year undergraduates and students at teacher training colleges. Although it can be used as a self-contained course, the book is primarily intended to serve as an introduction to English syntax for students who wish to pursue the subject further. We believe that it can serve a useful purpose not only for students who go on to study more comprehensive grammars such as Randolph Quirk et al., *A Grammar of Contemporary English* (London, 1972), but also for those who wish to study English syntax in the framework of a particular linguistic theory.

The book has four aims:

1. to introduce students to the categories and principal structures of English syntax;
2. to teach them how to recognize and analyse these categories and structures;
3. to provide them with a descriptive method and a terminology which, within the book's limited scope, are as explicit and consistent as possible;
4. to develop their skill in syntactic argumentation.

The book consists of two parts, preceded by an INTRODUCTION. The introduction deals with linguistic descriptions in general and with some key notions in syntactic analysis. PART ONE is devoted to the units of grammatical description, PART TWO to structures. In A GUIDE TO SENTENCE ANALYSIS, examples are given to illustrate how sentences can be analysed. The terminology employed is mainly traditional and familiar, but we have introduced a few new terms which we consider necessary to achieve our aim of descriptive consistency.

We would like to emphasize that this book does not claim to be comprehensive nor does it pretend to offer solutions to all descriptive problems. In fact, it deliberately ignores problems that arise in the border area between syntax and semantics. However, if it contributes at all to making students aware of the fact that English syntax is an area with many unresolved and controversial issues, we shall be satisfied.

The text of this book has been tested in the classroom over a number of years in several Departments of English, both in Holland and elsewhere. As a result it has gone through a number of revisions which we hope have enhanced its readability and removed some of its shortcomings. We are grateful for the detailed comments we have received from our Nijmegen colleagues as well as from many others in the Departments of English of the

Universities of Utrecht, Amsterdam, Groningen, Gent, Leuven and Olden-
burg. Their criticisms have led to a large number of improvements. Where
we have not followed their suggestions, the responsibility is obviously ours.
Special thanks go to Professor Randolph Quirk for permission to make use
of the files of The Survey of English Usage and for his hospitality during the
time we spent doing research at University College London. Our indebted-
ness to *A Grammar of Contemporary English* should be obvious to anyone
who is familiar with that book. We are also very much obliged to Mr R. A.
Close, Honorary Research Fellow of University College London, who
meticulously read through the whole text and from whose many critical
remarks this book has benefited a great deal. Finally, we must thank Vera
Kleerekoper, Mies Faber and Diane Crook for their patience and for the
skill with which they invariably succeeded in converting messy handwriting
into beautiful typescript.

Department of English   F.A.   J.A.
University of Nijmegen
Erasmusplein 1,
6500 HD Nijmegen,
Holland.

This reprint contains a number of minor corrections and improvements,
which result from critical remarks made by our reviewers.

Nijmegen, May 1986   F.A. J.A.

Contents

Introduction

This book is an introduction to the syntax of present-day written English, more particularly to the variety known as Standard British English. Its scope is best defined by a brief discussion of some of the ways in which a language can be described. These are dealt with in section 0.1. In section 0.2 a survey is given of the linguistic units in terms of which English syntax can be treated.

0.1 The goals of linguistic descriptions

Linguistics has roughly two goals: the description of human language in general and the description of individual languages like German, French or English. Each description of an individual language may be looked upon as a contribution to the study of language in general. One of the most interesting problems that linguists have occupied themselves with is the question whether the study of individual languages can throw light on the existence of 'linguistic universals', that is properties that all human languages are supposed to share. However interesting such questions may be, they are not the concern of this book.

The description of a language like English may be undertaken for several reasons. The most important distinction to be made here is that between descriptions that treat language as rule-governed behaviour and those that are pedagogically orientated. Many linguists claim that the goal of a linguistic description is to make explicit what the native speaker-listener knows about his language. This knowledge (his 'linguistic competence') may be defined as the set of rules that enable him to produce and to understand grammatically correct sentences. Others insist that linguistics should also account for 'communicative competence', that is for the fact that speakers also know how to use sentences that are socially appropriate. Both these goals are theoretical in the sense that the description is not primarily undertaken to serve some practical purpose, but to gain a better understanding of the nature and complexity of language.

Not every description of English, however, is an attempt to specify the rules that native speakers use in constructing and interpreting English sentences. Pedagogical grammars, for instance, serve a different purpose. Their main goal is to enable foreign students to learn the language rather than to provide insight into questions of a theoretical nature. Pedagogical grammars of English, in other words, supply information about the facts without offering detailed explanations of why these facts are as they are. For

1

example, whereas a pedagogical grammar should state that the members of pairs like

(1) a. It is likely that John will pass his examination
    b. John is likely to pass his examination

and

(2) a. All students should read that book
    b. That book should be read by all students

have the same meaning, a theoretically orientated grammar should try to offer some explanation for these facts.

Pedagogical grammars play an important part in the student's linguistic education. Apart from their role in language acquisition they form the basis on which the student's further, more theoretical, linguistic training can be founded. Students who have studied pedagogical grammars may be supposed to *know* English. They do not yet *know about* English. This book makes an attempt to take them beyond that first stage.

0.1.1 *Diachronic and synchronic descriptions*

Linguistic descriptions differ also with respect to their historical orientation. Every language has a history and the linguist can therefore adopt either a diachronic or a synchronic approach.

A **diachronic description** of English is concerned with the evolution of the language through time, that is with the changes it has undergone in its sound-system, its syntax and its vocabulary. What historical linguists are interested in are questions like the following:

'How do we explain the change from Old English *cyning*, *dæg* and *hlāf* to present-day English *king*, *day* and *loaf*?'

'Why is it that constructions like *I hym folwed* ('I followed him'), *Me was toold* ('I was told') and *Wyl þe lettyr was in wrytyng* ('While the letter was being written') were regularly found in Middle English, but are ungrammatical today?'

'How do we account for the fact that many English words have either lost one or more of the meanings they used to have (for example, in the seventeenth century *mutton* could mean 'prostitute' and *pretty* could be a synonym of *brave*) or have acquired new meanings (the word *grass*, for example, can now mean 'marijuana' and *to dig* can mean 'to like' or 'to understand')?

A **synchronic description** does not deal with historical change, but with what the Swiss linguist Ferdinand de Saussure called an *état de langue*. By this he meant that the synchronic study of language is not interested in linguistic evolution, but only in a particular 'language state', that is the language system as it presents itself at a particular time in its history. The label 'synchronic' does not necessarily refer to the contemporary language, but may also denote an earlier stage. A synchronic description of English may thus be a description of the language as it is written and spoken today, but also of the English of the time of Shakespeare or Charles Dickens. This book is only concerned with the description of present-day English.

0.1.2 *Varieties of English*

There are several reasons why a language like English cannot be viewed as homogeneous. In the first place, no two speakers of English speak in exactly the same way. Every individual speaker employs a variety of the language (known as his 'idiolect') that is uniquely his own, containing features that do not occur anywhere else. Moreover, apart from idiolects, it is necessary to take account of varieties that are determined by factors such as the speaker's geographical origin, social status, profession, education, age, sex, etc. Strictly speaking, therefore, there is no such thing as 'the English Language'. Linguists agree that it is more realistic to speak of 'varieties of English'.

Linguistic descriptions naturally differ with respect to the variety of language they are concerned with. Among the geographical varieties we can distinguish are British English, American English, Canadian English, Australian English and New Zealand English. In Great Britain we find a standard language and a number of non-standard, less prestigious, local dialects, such as Yorkshire English, Tyneside English and Cockney. Standard British English, as the name implies, is a dialect that has been 'standardized'. This means that, as a result of economic, political and other factors, it is recognized as *the* variety of the language and has consequently acquired more prestige than the other dialects. In Great Britain it is a non-localized variety used by most educated speakers. It is also the language of the schools, of the press and of most radio and television programmes.

Equally important in this connection is the distinction between spoken English and written (or printed) English. Traditionally linguistics has tended to concentrate on the description of the language of printed documents and to neglect the spoken language, in particular its syntax. One of the reasons was that the spoken language was considered to be less formal and therefore less worthy of attention than the written language. But of course it is also considerably more difficult to describe, as any attempt to analyse a tape-recorded conversation will show. Linguists are now beginning to pay more and more attention to the description of spoken English. For the time being, however, descriptions of English are likely to remain solidly based on the written variety of the language.

It is obvious that no description of English can deal with all varieties at the same time. In this book we chiefly concentrate on the written variety of Standard British English.

0.1.3 *Levels of analysis*

Within the limits outlined above the scope of a linguistic description can be narrowed still further by confining it to a particular **level of linguistic analysis**. If it is the task of the linguist to make explicit what the native speaker-listener knows about his language, then what he should explain is how speakers encode messages (that is how they pair meanings with sounds) and how listeners decode messages (that is how they pair sounds with meanings). This is an extremely difficult task which can be simplified to some extent by setting up levels of linguistic analysis. These facilitate the description in that they enable the linguist to focus his attention on one particular aspect of the language he is investigating. Although there is no consensus of opinion on the number of levels to be distinguished, it has been customary to set up at least four levels for English: the **sound level**, the **morphological level**, the **syntactic level** and the **semantic level**.

At the sound level the linguist is first of all concerned with the study of human speech sounds in general. This is the business of **phonetics**, which, in principle, studies all speech sounds, not just those of a particular language. Phoneticians are chiefly interested in questions like the following:

1. what is the range of human speech sounds?
2. how are they produced?
3. how are they transmitted?
4. how are they received?
5. how can they be classified?

Different languages make different selections from the total range of human speech sounds. The study of the selection made by a particular language and of the systematic functioning of the selected items in that language is the task of **phonology**. Phonology thus differs from phonetics in being language-specific. For example, whereas the phonetician is interested in all the different *k*-sounds that the speech organs can produce, the phonologist wants to know which of these occur in English and how they function in the English phonological system: do they discriminate meanings or not and in what environments do they occur?

Unlike the sound level, the morphological level of analysis is concerned with meaningful units. These units are called morphemes, which may be defined as the smallest meaningful units of grammatical description, since they cannot by analysed any further at this level. **Morphology** studies the internal structure of words, that is the ways in which morphemes function as constituents of word structure. For example, the word *unconditionally* may be said to consist of four morphemes: *un - condition - al - ly*. *Condition* is a free morpheme, since it can occur on its own. The other three morphemes are bound, since they must always co-occur with free morphemes. English words consist of one or more free morphemes (*book, bookcase, bookshop, bookworm*) or of combinations of free and bound morphemes (*kindness, unkind, kindly, unkindly*).

Having established the structure of words at the morphological level, we can go on to examine how words can be put together to form larger grammatical units. It is evident that a language is not simply an inventory of words. Words combine to form larger units called phrases, which, in turn, combine to form sentences. It is the task of **syntax** to establish the set of rules that specify which combinations of words constitute grammatical strings and which do not. The following are examples of simple syntactic rules in English (the asterisk denotes an ungrammatical string):

The definite article precedes the noun: the book
*book the

A relative clause follows its antecedent: the girl that you told me about
*the that you told me about girl

Negative sentences with *not* require the auxiliary *do* (if they do not contain an auxiliary): I do not know him
*I know him not

The verb *want* must be followed by a non-finite clause: I want you to go
*I want that you go

Apart from their phonological make-up and their syntactic structure, sentences have a meaning aspect: they convey messages. A linguistic description which ignores meaning is obviously incomplete. The study of meaning is the concern of the semantic level of linguistic analysis. Thus it is the task of the semanticist to explain why sentences like *Jim owns this car* and *This car belongs to Jim* are felt to be synonymous, why a sentence like *Are you looking for the glasses?* is ambiguous, why *Bachelors are not married* is tautological and why *That boy is my sister* is a contradiction. **Semantics** investigates the meanings of individual words as well as the meanings of whole sentences. It is important to emphasize this point since the meaning of a sentence is not simply the sum total of the meanings of the words it contains. The following examples show that it is possible for two sentences to contain the same words with the same meanings, but to signal entirely different messages:

(3) I would like to marry you
(4) I would like you to marry

What kind of message is conveyed obviously depends not only on the meaning of individual lexical items but also on syntactic structure. That is why it is anything but easy (and indeed many linguists claim that it is impossible) to separate syntax from semantics. However, these are problems which are beyond the scope of this book.

Figure 1 shows that each of the linguistic levels discussed above has a corresponding component in the **grammar** (that is the total linguistic description) of the language.

This book is not a complete grammar in the above sense of the word. Although there are occasional comments on phonological and semantic

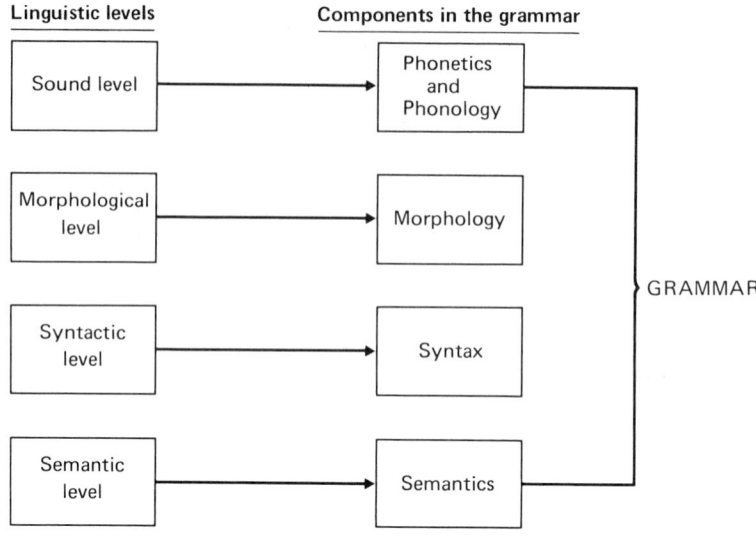

Figure 1

matters, we have little to say on sounds and meanings. Our main concern is with morphology and syntax.

0.2 Linguistic units and the sentence

The description of the various components of a grammar has always concentrated on different sorts of linguistic units. Semantic descriptions, for example, have tended to concentrate on the meaning of individual words, and have only recently begun to pay attention to larger units than the word. Syntactic descriptions, on the other hand, have traditionally taken the **sentence** as their starting-point, smaller units being primarily regarded as 'building-blocks' of sentences. Since in this book we are in the first place concerned with syntax, we shall mainly deal with sentences and with smaller units as component parts of sentences.

Sentences consist of words. However, nobody would look upon (5a) as a sentence, although it is a string of eight English words:

(5) a. Lion cage this less in dangerous is the

Now, if we compare (5a) with:

(5) b. The lion is less dangerous in this cage

we will unhesitatingly accept the latter example as a sentence. It is true that in (5a) we are able to assign some sort of meaning to each word individually, but we fail to make any sense of the sequence as a whole; (5a), in other words, is not meaningful, whereas (5b) is. We shall therefore say that, if a sequence of words is to constitute a sentence, it must be meaningful.

0.2.1 *Wordorder and sentence structure*

The reason why we cannot make sense of (5a) is that we cannot tell which words should be grouped together. In (5b), on the other hand, it is perfectly obvious that *less* combines with *dangerous* to form *less dangerous*, rather than with *is* to form *is less*. Similarly *the* combines with *lion*, *this* with *cage*, and *in* with *this cage*. Thus, in (5b) we have three coherent groups of words: *the lion*, *less dangerous* and *in this cage*. Apart from being internally coherent, these groups also stand in a certain relation to each other. Thus *less dangerous* combines primarily with *the lion* rather than with *in this cage*. The latter group relates to the combination *the lion is less dangerous* as a whole. This network of relations between the words of a sentence is called its **structure**.

As appears from a comparison of (5a) and (5b), one of the factors that determines the structure of a sentence is the order in which the words are arranged. It is obvious that this order is subject to strict rules. For example, if in (5b) we keep *the lion* in initial position and examine the possibilities of arranging the other groups, we find that only (5f) has an acceptable wordorder:

(5) b.   The lion is less dangerous in this cage
    c.   *The lion is in this cage less dangerous
    d.   *The lion less dangerous in this cage is
    e.   *The lion less dangerous is in this cage
    f.   The lion in this cage is less dangerous
    g.   *The lion in this cage less dangerous is

The importance of the role played by **wordorder** appears not only from the unacceptability of four out of the six examples above, but also from the fact that the different order of the words in the two acceptable sentences (5b) and (5f) entails a difference in their structure and in their meaning. In (5f) *in this cage* now primarily combines with *the lion*, whereas *less dangerous* relates to the combination *the lion in this cage* as a whole. The difference in meaning is that in (5b) a particular lion (that the speaker has been talking about) is said to be less dangerous in this cage (than in another), but that in (5f) the lion in this cage is said to be less dangerous (than other lions in other cages). Other examples of the crucial part played by wordorder are the following pairs of sentences. In each pair the difference in wordorder results in a difference in structure as well as in meaning:

(6) a.   Did he say who he was?
    b.   Who did he say he was?
(7) a.   He wanted to marry Jane
    b.   He wanted Jane to marry
(8) a.   I'll have it copied within a minute
    b.   I'll have copied it within a minute
(9) a.   Who has John rung up?
    b.   Who has rung up John?

To comment only on the last pair, it is clear that in (9a) the agent of the action denoted by the verb is *John* and that *who* inquires after the identity of the person that John rang up. In (9b) *who* inquires after the agent of the action and it is John who has been rung up.

Differences in wordorder need not always have the effect that they have in sentences (6–9). In spite of differences in wordorder, we assign identical structures and identical meanings to the (a) and (b) sentences below:

(10) a. John ran away
     b. Away ran John
(11) a. On the horizon appeared a lonely horseman
     b. A lonely horseman appeared on the horizon
(12) a. I fail to understand this problem
     b. This problem I fail to understand

It will be noticed that in sentences (6–9) wordorder differences entail differences in the logical relationships between words and groups of words. This is not the case, however, in sentences (10–12), where these relationships remain constant and the different wordorder merely brings about a shift in emphasis.

0.2.2 *Word-meaning and sentence structure*

So far we have discussed sentence structure in terms of wordorder, giving examples of pairs of sentences containing the same words, and we have seen that a difference in wordorder often results in a difference in structure and meaning. Wordorder, however, is not the only factor that determines sentence structure. The structure of a sentence also depends on the individual meanings of the words or word-groups making up the sentence. Consider:

(13) a. He looked up the number
     b. He looked up the chimney
(14) a Mary was waiting for two friends
     b. Mary was waiting for two minutes
(15) a. You shouldn't have left him so ill
     b. You shouldn't have left him so early
(16) a. She made him a good wife
     b. She made him a good dinner
(17) a. Peter had dreamt the whole night
     b. Peter had dreamt the whole story

In each pair the (a) and (b) sentences have different structures. This cannot be due to wordorder, but must be attributed to the fact that the last words are different and, consequently, contribute different meanings to the total meaning of the whole sentence. That the structures of the (a) and (b) sentences are different appears, for example, from the fact that in (13a) there is a close relation between *look* and *up*, which is absent in (13b); here we recognize a relation between *up* and *the chimney*. Again, in (14a) *for* goes with *waiting*, whereas in (14b) it combines with *two minutes*. Other structural differences can be detected in (15–17).

0.2.3 *Structural ambiguity*

Our examples so far have been ones in which structure is overtly indicated by wordorder (6–9) or by different lexical items (13–17). Sentence structure is, however, not always unambiguously derivable from overt marks like these, as can be seen from so-called ambiguous sentences like the following:

(18) Visiting relatives can be boring
(19) Freddy likes Susan more than Joan

An **ambiguous sentence** is one to which we can assign more than one structure and therefore more than one meaning. Thus (19) allows of the following two interpretations:

(19) a. Freddy likes Susan more than Freddy likes Joan
     b. Freddy likes Susan more than Joan likes Susan

The absence of any overt clues in sentence (19) makes it impossible for us to say whether it should be interpreted as (19a) or as (19b). Such structural ambiguities cannot be solved, then, by looking at the sentence in isolation. When the sentence is embedded in a larger context, however, the context will usually provide clues indicating which of the two readings is the intended one.

Summarizing the major points of what has been said so far, we can say that:

1. if a sequence of words is to constitute a sentence, it must be meaningful;
2. sentences are interpreted not as strings of individual words but as sequences of groups of words;
3. between the words and word-groups of a sentence there exist certain relations;
4. the network of relations between the words and word-groups of a sentence is called its structure;
5. clues to the structure of a sentence can be found in its wordorder and in the meanings of the words in the sentence;
6. although wordorder provides a significant clue to the structure of a sentence, sentence structure is not always observed in the linear sequence of the words in the sentence.

0.2.4 *The notation of sentence structure*

Since sentence structure is not always directly observable in the written form of sentences, we need a special notational device to make the structure of sentences 'visible'. There are two devices for the notation of sentence structure: **diagramming** or **bracketing**. To take diagramming first, the structure of

(20) John took a walk

may be represented as in Figure 2 or Figure 3:

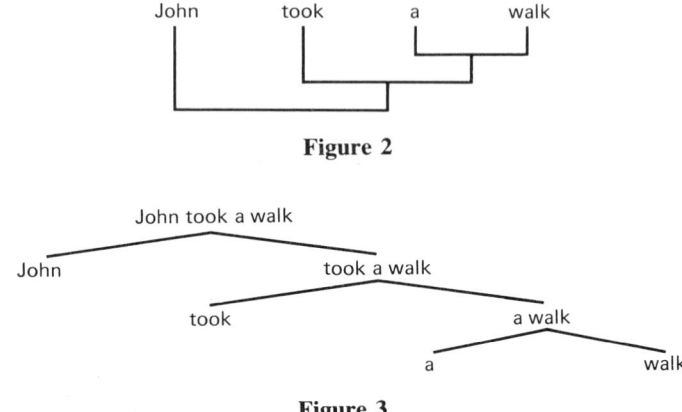

Figure 2

Figure 3

The second device employs brackets to indicate structure:

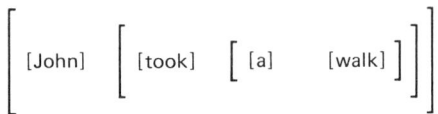

Figure 4

Each of the above notations represent the sentence as consisting of two major parts: *John* and *took a walk*, the second of which is again divisible into two parts *took* and *a walk*, while the latter part falls apart into *a* and *walk*. The notations in Figures 2 and 3 are known as **tree-diagrams**, the difference being that 2 proceeds from the smaller segments towards the sentence as a whole, whereas 3 takes the whole sentence as a starting-point, gradually analysing it into smaller segments. Since the tree-diagram of Figure 3 is easier to read as a visual representation of the structure of the sentence, we shall use this notation rather than those of Figures 2 and 4.

0.2.5 *Constituents*

The parts into which a sentence can be segmented are the **constituents** of the sentence. The term **immediate constituents** (IC's) refers to those constituents which together form a higher-order constituent. In our example, *a* and *walk* are the IC's of *a walk*, *took* and *a walk* are the IC's of *took a walk*, while *John* and *took a walk* are the two IC's of the sentence. Since the sentence is commonly regarded as the largest unit of syntactic description,

John took a walk cannot be said to be an IC of anything. It is true, of course, that certain relations obtain between a sentence and the context in which it occurs, but these relations are of a different order from the sentence-internal relations with which a syntactic description is concerned.

0.2.6 *Phrases, words and morphemes*

Although constituents can be regarded as elements that play a role in larger structures we can also look upon them as linguistic units in their own right. If we do not consider units like *John*, *took* and *a walk* as sentence constituents but as independent linguistic objects that have their own characteristics (such as their own internal structure), we call them **phrases**. Phrases do not resemble sentences (*John*, *took* and *a walk* are not sentences), although it is their natural function to serve as constituents of sentences. Phrases may consist of single words (*John*, *took*) or of more words (*a walk*). Almost every phrase can be lengthened by adding more words. In doing so, we change the internal structure of the phrase, but not the structure of the sentence of which it is a constituent. We might, for example, lengthen *John* to *young John*, replace *took* by *may have taken*, and *a walk* by *a walk through the woods*, but this would not affect the structure of our example sentence.

It is clear that phrases like *may have taken* and *a walk through the woods* do not belong to the same type; the former is called a **verb phrase**, the latter a **noun phrase**. As these examples show, phrases are called by the name of the word class to which all their constituents belong (*may*, *have* and *taken* are all verbs), or by the name of the word class to which their most dominant constituent belongs (*walk* is a noun). The following types of phrase are distinguished (for a more detailed discussion of phrases see Chapter 3):

noun phrase	eg:	*a walk, a walk through the woods*
verb phrase	eg:	*took, may have taken*
adjective phrase	eg:	*very young, too young to marry*
adverb phrase	eg:	*seriously, quite seriously*
prepositional phrase	eg:	*at the corner, at the corner of the street*

As we have seen, phrases are composed of **words**, and a minimal phrase consists of one single word. However, in the same way that we can look upon a phrase as a linguistic unit in its own right, we can examine a word not as a constituent of a phrase, but as an independent linguistic unit. And just as we can distinguish between different phrase types, we can distinguish between different word types or, as they are more commonly called, **word classes**, such as noun, verb, adjective, etc. One way to examine the word as an individual unit is to leave the field of syntax and enter that of morphology, by looking at the constituents of which words are composed. We saw above that a word like *unconditionally* may be said to consist of four units: *un-, condition, -al* and *-ly*. These units are called **morphemes;** *condition* is called a free morpheme because it can also function independently as a word, while the other three are called bound morphemes, since they must always be combined with at least one free morpheme. Like a minimal phrase a minimal word consists of just one constituent; this is always a free morpheme. Within the scope of the present description we only consider morphemes as constituents of words; we are not concerned with the morpheme as an individual unit with its own constituent structure, since this would lead us into the field of phonology.

0.2.7 *Rankscale and rankshift*

We have now established a hierarchy of units of linguistic description: morphemes function as constituents of words, words function as constituents of phrases, and phrases as constituents of sentences. This hierarchy has been called the **rankscale**; it is illustrated in Figure 5.

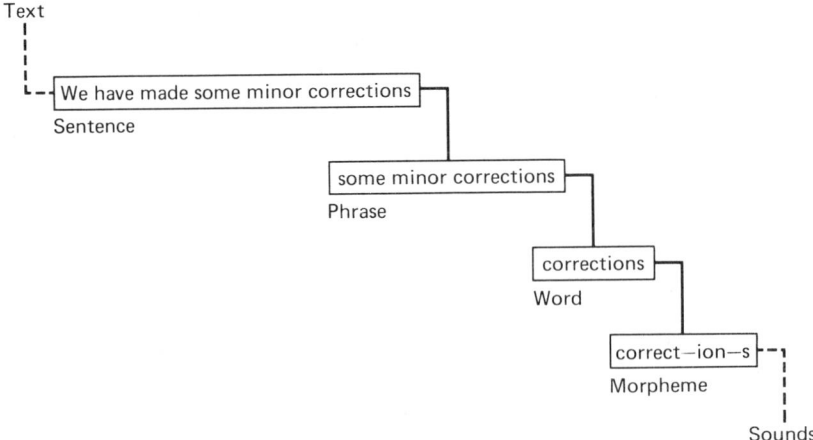

Figure 5

However, units are not always consistently composed of units of the next lowest rank. Quite frequently, a unit of a given rank functions as a constituent of a unit of the same rank or even of a unit which is one step lower down the rankscale; this phenomenon has been called **rankshift**. Thus it is possible for sentences to function as constituents of other sentences and even as constituents of phrases. Phrases may be constituents of other phrases and words may function in the structure of other words. This is illustrated in Figure 6, where the left side of the figure illustrates the normal hierarchy of units and the right side indicates rankshift possibilities:

Examples:

(21) I know *Peter is in the army*
(22) (I am) very pleased *you could come*
(23) at the corner *of the street*
(24) treetop; goldsmith; blackbird

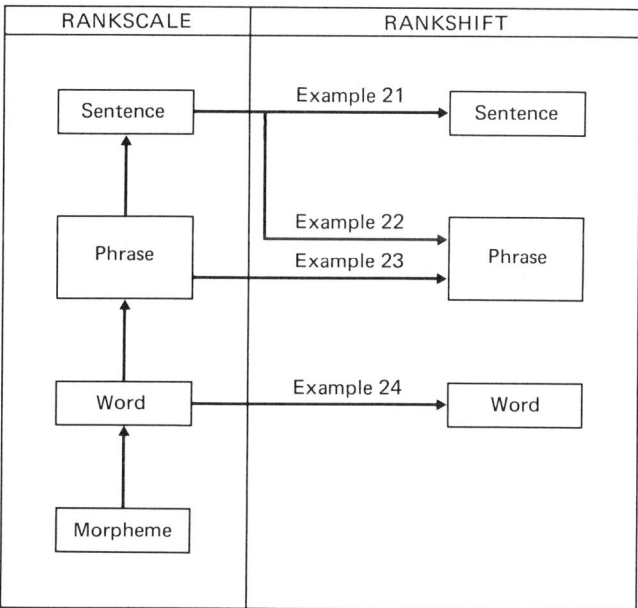

Figure 6

0.2.8 *Functions and categories*

We have made a distinction between linguistic units as constituents of larger structures and as linguistic objects in their own right. These two aspects can be observed with most linguistic units. With the exception of the sentence, every unit, at every level of analysis, can be considered either as an element that plays a role in a larger structure, or as something that has its own individual characteristics—in the same way that we may look upon an individual person either as, say, a teacher, a father or an English citizen, or as someone who is tall, bald or wears glasses. If we view a linguistic unit as an element that plays its role in a larger linguistic structure, we are concerned with its **function**; if we view it as something that has individual characteristics which it shares with other units of the same kind, we are concerned with the **category** or **class** to which it belongs. Returning to our example sentence, we can look at the units *John* and *walk* individually and observe that they are both nouns and therefore belong to the same category or word class. We can also look at *John* and *a walk* individually and conclude that they are both noun phrases and therefore, again, categorically equivalent. If, however, we look at *John* and *a walk* as constituents of the sentence, we observe that their functions are different: *John* functions as subject and *a walk* functions as direct object of the sentence. This example shows that there is not necessarily a one-to-one correspondence between functions and categories; not only may the same category realize different functions, but the same function may be realized by different categories. We have already seen that two noun phrases (*John* and *a walk*) may realize two different functions in one and the same sentence. In the following examples the noun phrase *next week* realizes four different functions:

(25) He leaves *next week*
(26) *Next week* is the time to do it
(27) Let's call *next week* period A
(28) Suppose we give *next week* priority

In the next two examples, on the other hand, the same function (that of direct object) is realized by different categories, a noun phrase and a (rankshifted) sentence respectively:

(29) He understood *the problem*
(30) He understood *what I was talking about*

Even though there is no one-to-one correspondence between categories and functions, it is true that most categories have a typical function associated with them. Typical functions of noun phrases are, for instance, those of subject and direct object, while the verb phrase is associated with the function predicator (on sentence functions see Chapter 7).

In this book a great deal of attention is paid to the category-function dichotomy. Part One is mainly concerned with the categories of the units of linguistic description. The order of the chapters reflects the rankscale hierarchy: the morpheme (Chapter 1), the word (Chapter 2), the phrase (Chapter 3) and the sentence (Chapter 4). In Part Two the emphasis is on structures. Here the units of linguistic description are examined with respect to their internal structure as well as with respect to the ways in which they function as constituents in larger structures. Again, the rankscale order is followed; since the internal structure of the morpheme falls outside the scope of this book, Chapter 5 deals with the structure of the word and Chapter 6 examines the structure of the phrase. The discussion of the sentence is divided over two chapters; in Chapter 7 the structure of the sentence is discussed, while Chapter 8 deals with the relation between sentence functions and the categories by which these functions may be realized.

Part One

The Units of Grammatical Description

1. The morpheme

The **morpheme** is the minimal unit of grammatical description in the sense that it cannot be segmented any further at the grammatical level of analysis. The word *unfriendly*, for example, is composed of three morphemes, since we can distinguish three irreducible elements, viz. *un-*, *friend* and *-ly*. These morphemes obviously belong to different categories in that *friend* can be used independently, whereas *un-* and *-ly* cannot. *Friend* is therefore a so-called **free morpheme**, *un-* and *-ly* being **bound morphemes**. In the structure of the word *unfriendly* the free morpheme *friend* is the root (*friendly* is the base, from which *unfriendly* is derived; on the difference between root and base see p. 101.

In English most roots are free morphemes. However, there are a number of English words whose roots are bound morphemes, since they cannot occur independently. Examples are the second elements in:

con - ceive	con - tain	con - fer
re - ceive	re - tain	re - fer
de - ceive	de - tain	de - fer

With respect to bound morphemes it is necessary to consider the concept of the allomorph. We shall illustrate this by first looking at the way nouns are pluralized in English. The plural of English nouns can be said to be formed by means of a plural morpheme, which may be represented as $\{s_1\}$ (where the subscript 1 serves to distinguish the plural morpheme from the genitive morpheme $\{s_2\}$). As appears from the examples in Table 1.1, $\{s_1\}$ has a number of phonological variants, depending on the environment in which it appears. These variants are called **allomorphs**. There are some nouns in English, such as *deer* and *sheep*, which do not change their form in the plural. In such cases we can say that the plural morpheme is realized by a zero allomorph, represented as $/\phi/$. Note that morphemes are enclosed within braces, allomorphs within slant lines.

Table 1.1

Plural morpheme	Allomorphs	Examples
$\{s_1\}$	/s/ /z/ /ɪz/ /ən/ /φ/	*hat*-/s/ *dog*-/z/ *bus*-/ɪz/ *ox*-/ən/ *deer*-/φ/

A second example to illustrate the concept of the allomorph is provided by words like *intolerable, impossible, illegible* and *irresponsible* (see Table

1.2). If we compare these with their positive counterparts, *tolerable*, *possible*, *legible* and *responsible*, we can say that their first element is a phonological variant of the negative morpheme {in}:

Table 1.2

Negative morpheme	Allomorphs	Examples
{in}	/ɪn/ /ɪl/ /ɪm/ /ɪr/ /ɪŋ/	/ɪn/-*tolerable*, /ɪn/-*active* /ɪl/-*legible*, /ɪl/-*logical* /ɪm/-*possible*, /ɪm/-*mobile* /ɪr/-*responsible*, /ɪr/-*regular* /ɪŋ/-*competent*, /ɪŋ/-*capable*

Apart from /ɪŋ/, *competent* and *capable* allow the allomorph /ɪn/.

Bound morphemes like {s₁} and {in} are called **affixes.** Affixes which are added to the beginning of a word are **prefixes,** affixes which are added to the end of a word are **suffixes.** Affixes are either inflexional or derivational.

Table 1.3

MORPHEME				
	Free	Root ———————		eg: ask, boy, example, great know, museum, run, strange
	Bound	AFFIX	Prefix → derivation ———	eg: a- : amoral de- : defrost ex- : ex-wife in- : insane mini- : mini-skirt non- : non-committal out- : outlive pre- : pre-cook re- : reclaim
			Suffix → derivation ———	eg: -able : readable -dom : kingdom -er : employer -hood : childhood -ity : nationality -less : careless -ness : largeness -ship : friendship
			→ inflexion ———	plural : boys genitive : boy's present tense 3rd person singular : asks past tense : asked -ed participle : asked -ing participle : asking comparative : greater superlative : greatest

Inflexional affixes mark such distinctions as the singular/plural contrast in nouns (*book: book-s*), the present tense/past tense contrast in verbs (*walk: walk-ed*) or the positive/comparative contrast in adjectives (*small: small-er*). **Derivational affixes** are added to the root or stem in order to produce a new word (*book: book-let, walk: walk-er, small: small-ness*). Prefixes are always derivational and many of them are non-class-changing. Suffixes are either derivational or inflexional; the majority of derivational suffixes are class-changing. The above distinctions are summarized in Table 1.3.

2. The word

2.1 Introductory

Words can be grouped together into **word classes** (also called **parts of speech**). If we assign words to the same class we imply that they share a number of properties. Word class membership may be said to depend on at least two kinds of properties: morphological and syntactic.

The class to which a word belongs can be established on morphological grounds if the word in question has inflexional and/or derivational characteristics that are typical of that class. Thus words that belong to the class of verbs generally take the inflexional endings -*s*, -*ing* and -*ed*. Typical inflexional endings for nouns are -*s* and '*s*. Typical endings of adjectives are the comparative and superlative endings -*er* and -*est*. Although these suffixes can also be added to some adverbs (eg *hard* and *fast*) they cannot.be said to be characteristic of the adverb class. The same three classes also contain many members that are derivationally identifiable. Thus words ending in -*ify* and -*ize* are verbs, words ending in -*ation*, -*ity* and -*ness* are nouns and words that are formed by the suffixes -*able*, -*ish* and -*less* are adjectives. Typical suffixes of the class of adverbs are -*ward(s)* and -*wise*. Some examples are given in Table 2.1.

Syntactic properties of word classes are reflected by the typical ways in which their members function in sentences and phrases. Thus verbs are typically associated with the sentence function predicator (see subsection 7.3.1), nouns with the functions subject (see section 7.2) and object (see subsections 7.3.2.1–7.3.2.3), adjectives with the functions subject attribute and object attribute (see subsections 7.3.2.4–7.3.2.5) and adverbs with the function adverbial (see section 7.4). Moreover, on a lower level, adjectives play a characteristic role in the structure of noun phrases (see subsection 6.1.2), adverbs in the structure of adjective and adverb phrases (see subsections 6.2.1 and 6.3.1).

Attempts have been made to identify word classes on the basis of semantic criteria. Thus nouns have traditionally been defined as words denoting persons, animals, plants, objects, etc. Verbs have been defined as words denoting actions, states and processes, adjectives as words referring to qualities. Semantic criteria, however, are, on the whole, less reliable indicators of word class membership than morphological and syntactic ones. For example, if we were to apply the above definitions to words like *handshake* and *death*, we would have to assign them to the class of verbs (rather than to the class of nouns), since they may be said to refer to an action and a state, respectively. Similarly, words like *roundness* and *strength*

Table 2.1

Word class	Inflexional endings	Typical derivational endings	
Verbs	*walk-s* (3rd pers. sg. pres. tense) *walk-ing* (*-ing* participle) *walk-ed* (past tense) *walk-ed* (*-ed* participle)	*ampl-ify* *cod-ify* *divers-ify* *simpl-ify* *typ-ify*	*legal-ize* *modern-ize* *popular-ize* *rational-ize* *symbol-ize*
Nouns	*boy-s* (plural) *boy's* (gen. sg.) *men's* (gen. pl.)	*complement-ation* *fix-ation* *found-ation* *relax-ation* *suffix-ation* *clever-ness* *dark-ness* *great-ness* *sly-ness* *sweet-ness*	*banal-ity* *dual-ity* *moral-ity* *partial-ity* *rapid-ity*
Adjectives	*great-er* (comparative) *great-est* (superlative)	*accept-able* *boy-ish* *eat-able* *child-ish* *kiss-able* *fool-ish* *read-able* *green-ish* *work-able* *self-ish*	*count-less* *fruit-less* *life-less* *thought-less* *top-less*
Adverbs	*hard-er* (comparative) *hard-est* (superlative)	*after-wards* *back-ward(s)* *down-ward(s)* *east-ward(s)* *up-ward(s)*	*clock-wise* *crab-wise* *cross-wise* *length-wise* *other-wise*

would have to be called adjectives (rather than nouns), since they denote qualities.

In view of the above we attach greater importance to morphological and syntactic criteria than to semantic ones. We consider syntactic criteria to take precedence over morphological ones since the morphology of English words does not always enable us to assign them to a particular class. In the first place there are numerous English words whose morphological shape does not provide any clue to their possible classification. Examples are words like *brief*, *fly*, *lack*, *tear* and *walk*. Secondly, there are several affixes which cannot unambiguously be associated with a particular word class. Thus the suffix *-ly* does not necessarily mark a word as belonging to the class of adverbs (cf adjectives like *lively*, *lovely* and *seemly*) nor does a suffix like *-er* characterize a word as a compared adjective (cf words like *cooler* and *drier*, which are either adjectives or nouns).

Many English words, if considered in isolation, cannot be classified as belonging to this or that word class. It is only when we consider their function in a particular context that we are able to say to which part of speech they belong. If a word is felt to belong primarily to class *X*, but is used in a function associated with members of class *Y*, we refer to the phenomenon in question as **conversion**. Thus words like *sir* and *inevitable* primarily belong to the class of nouns and adjectives, respectively. However, they may be said to be converted into a verb and a noun in contexts like:

Don't sir me, please

We are prepared for the inevitable to happen

In many cases words are not felt to belong primarily to one particular class *X*, but to more than one class at the same time. For instance, it is hard to tell whether words like *answer* and *desire* are primarily verbs or nouns. In such cases it is perhaps better to speak of **multiple membership** rather than of conversion. Some more examples are given in Table 2.2.

2.2 Word classes

It is possible to distinguish between major and minor word classes. The former are also called **open classes**; their membership is unrestricted and indefinitely large since they allow the addition of new members. Minor word classes are **closed classes**; their membership is restricted since they do not allow the creation of new members. Moreover, the number of items they comprise is, as a rule, so small that they can easily be listed. In English there are four major word classes: nouns, adjectives, adverbs and verbs. The minor word classes are: prepositions, conjunctions, articles, numerals, pronouns, quantifiers and interjections. We shall deal with each of these classes separately.

2.2.1 *Nouns*

Within the class of **nouns** we can distinguish members which are identifiable as nouns on the basis of typical derivational suffixes. Moreover, most nouns are morphologically characterized by their ability to take typical inflexional suffixes.

Typical derivational suffixes of nouns are:

-age	: anchorage, coverage, postage
-ance	: acceptance, appearance, utterance
-ation	: affirmation, information, transformation
-dom	: boredom, freedom, kingdom
-ee	: divorcee, employee, payee
-eer	: engineer, mountaineer, profiteer
-ence	: difference, existence, preference
-ess	: actress, governess, murderess
-ette	: cigarette, maisonette, usherette
-hood	: childhood, knighthood, parenthood
-ism	: idealism, modernism, organism
-ist	: Marxist, royalist, specialist
-ment	: amendment, commandment, shipment
-ness	: bitterness, exactness, whiteness
-ship	: friendship, kinship, scholarship

Table 2.2

	Noun	Verb	Adjective	Adverb	Preposition	Conjunction	Context
laugh	+	+					We had a good laugh over John's mistake Why do you laugh?
doubt	+	+					I have my doubts about his honesty I cannot doubt his honesty
dry		+	+				She was drying her hair Is this paint dry?
brave		+	+				We decided to brave the storm It was very brave of you to go
daily	+		+	+			*The Guardian* is a daily We all have to earn our daily bread This newspaper appears daily
since				+	+	+	I have not seen him since He has lived in London since the war I have known Jim since he came to live here
fast			+	+			My brother has bought a very fast car Why do you always drive so fast?
round	+	+	+	+	+		He was knocked out in the first round The police-car rounded the corner on two wheels We have a round table in our dining-room When will you come round again? The guard walked round the building

Most nouns can take two inflexional suffixes, one to mark number (the plural) and one to mark case (the genitive).

The plural

The plural morpheme {s₁} is regularly realized in three ways:

/s/   : after bases ending in voiceless sounds except sibilants, eg: books, roofs, lips, hats, births

/z/   : after bases ending in voiced sounds except sibilants, eg: trees, bars, laws, zoos, days, boys, ribs, beds, dogs, flames, pens, bottles

/ɪz/   : after bases ending in a sibilant:
   /s/   : horses, nurses, kisses
   /z/   : noises, sizes, noses
   /ʃ/   : brushes, dishes, clashes
   /ʒ/   : mirages
   /tʃ/ : churches, torches, witches
   /dʒ/ : pledges, bridges, languages

There are four exceptions to the pluralization rule formulated above:

1. Change in the base + regular suffix, eg:
   /θ/ → /ð/ + /z/ : baths, mouths, paths
   /f/ → /v/ + /z/ : halves, knives, thieves
   /s/ → /z/ + /ɪz/ : houses
2. Change in the base without a suffix (= mutation):
   foot   – feet   louse – lice   man   – men
   tooth – teeth   mouse – mice   woman – women
   goose – geese
3. No change (= zero plural), eg:
   deer   grouse   species   Chinese   Portuguese   (air)craft
   sheep salmon   series   Japanese Swiss
4. -en plural
   child – children (with mutation)
   ox   – oxen

The spelling of the regular plural of English nouns is -s or -es. The latter spelling is found in:

1. words ending in -s, -z, -ch, -sh and x, eg:
   gases, dresses, waltzes, matches, wishes, boxes;
2. many words ending in a consonant symbol + -o, eg:
   echoes, potatoes, tomatoes (but note: kilos, photos, pianos).

The spelling -(e)s is also found in the following two cases, where the spelling of the base is affected:

1. in words ending in a consonant symbol + -y, where y changes into i, eg:
   bodies, countries, flies;
2. in the following words, where the f of the base is changed into v:
   calves, halves, knives, lives, wives, leaves, sheaves, thieves, loaves,
   wolves, elves, selves, shelves.

Foreign words in English form their plural in three different ways.
First there are those that take a regular native plural, eg:

dilemma	– dilemmas	prospectus	– prospectuses
encyclopedia	– encyclopedias	virus	– viruses
museum	– museums	asylum	– asylums

Some foreign words take both a native and a foreign plural, eg:

formula	– formulas	– formulae
cactus	– cactuses	– cacti
syllabus	– syllabuses	– syllabi
index	– indexes	– indices
memorandum	– memorandums	– memoranda

Finally there are foreign words that take a foreign plural only, eg:

analysis	– analyses	desideratum	– desiderata
basis	– bases	erratum	– errata
diagnosis	– diagnoses	stratum	– strata
thesis	– theses	criterion	– criteria
alumnus	– alumni	phenomenon	– phenomena
stimulus	– stimuli		

The genitive

The **genitive** is one of the two cases of the English noun, the other being the
common (or unmarked) **case**.

In the singular the genitive morpheme $\{s_2\}$ is regularly realized in three
ways:

/s/   : after bases ending in voiceless sounds except sibilants, eg:

Dick	– Dick's car
ship	– the ship's crew
dentist	– the dentist's drill
wife	– his wife's lover

/z/   : after bases ending in voiced sounds except sibilants, eg:

Fred	– Fred's salary
play	– the play's title
brother	– my brother's cottage
firm	– the firm's losses

/ɪz/   : after bases ending in a sibilant, eg:

    horse   – a horse's tail
    Keats   – Keats's poetry
    George – George's children
    village – the village's population
    Church – the Church's teachings

Proper nouns ending in /z/ take either /ɪz/ or /φ/, the regular form being /ɪz/:

    Dickens – Dickens's(s) – 'dɪkɪnzɪz/'dɪkɪnz
    Forbes – Forbes's(s) – 'fɔːbzɪz/'fɔːbz

The genitive singular suffix is realized by /φ/ in two cases:

1. in a number of fixed expressions, eg:
for goodness' sake
for Jesus' sake
2. with Greek names of more than one syllable, eg:
Sophocles' plays
Xerxes' strategy

In the plural the genitive morpheme is realized in two ways:

/z/   : with irregular plurals not ending in -s:
    men – men's clothes   children – children's books
    women– women's lib

/φ/   : in all other cases, eg:
    boys   – a boys' school
    students – the students' union
    officers – the officers' mess
    teachers – a teachers' association

The spelling of the genitive suffix in both the singular and the plural is either *'s* or *'*. The possibilities and the relations between spelling and pronunciation are set out in Table 2.3.

Table 2.3

Genitive	Spelling	Pronunciation	Examples
Singular	's 's or ' '	/s/, /z/, /ɪz/ /ɪz/, /φ/ /φ/	*ship's*; *brother's*; *George's* *Dickens's(s)* *Xerxes'*
Plural	's '	/z/ /φ/	*men's*; *women's*; *children's* *boys'*; *students'*

Classes of nouns

Nouns can be subdivided into:

1. **common nouns**; these are further subdivided into **count nouns** and **mass nouns**;
2. **proper nouns**.

As Table 2.4 shows, this classification can be based on a number of syntactic criteria.

Table 2.4

		Plural	Numerals	*many, few several*	*much, little*	Def. article	Indef. article
Common	Count	+	+	+	−	+	+
	Mass	−	−	−	+	+	−
Proper		−	−	−	−	−	−

Proper nouns do not occur in the plural and cannot be preceded by numerals and by quantifiers such as *many, few, several, much* and *little*. Nor can they be preceded by the definite and indefinite articles. The subclassification of common nouns into count nouns and mass nouns is based on the fact that count nouns are positive with respect to five of the criteria used, whereas mass nouns are positive with respect to only two criteria: they collocate with the quantifiers *much* and *little* as well as with the definite article. Consider:

Criteria	*Examples*
Plural	count : chair – chairs, book – books
	mass : music – *musics, despair – *despairs
	proper : Eric – *Erics, France – *Frances
Numerals	count : two chairs, two books
	mass : *two musics, *two despairs
	proper : *two Erics, *two Frances
Many/few/several	count : many chairs, many books
	mass : *many musics, *many despairs
	proper : *many Erics, *many Frances
Much/little	count : *much chair, *much book
	mass : much music, much despair
	proper : *much Eric, *much France
Definite article	count : the chair, the book
	mass : the music, the despair
	proper : *the Eric, *the France
Indefinite article	count : a chair, a book
	mass : *a music, *a despair
	proper : *an Eric, *a France

Proper nouns normally have unique reference, that is they refer to one particular person, country, town, etc. This semantic property explains why they occur in the singular only and cannot be preceded by articles, numerals and quantifiers. Occasionally, however, proper nouns lose their unique reference, in which case they are treated as count nouns, so that they can be pluralized and be preceded by numerals, articles and by quantifiers like *many, few* and *several*:

I know two/several Erics
The France I used to know does not exist any more
Does your brother think he is a Rembrandt?

Just as proper nouns can be treated as count nouns, so can mass nouns:

Mass	*Count*
I am not fond of cheese	John likes French cheeses only
Coffee is expensive	Two coffees, please
We drink little wine	Let's buy a good wine next year
She has red hair	There is a hair in your soup
Many psychologists are interested in language	John speaks several languages
Don't make so much noise	They heard strange noises last night
There's egg on your chin	Do you like eggs?
That grammar is out of print	Hubert collects Japanese prints

2.2.2 *Adjectives*

Many members of the class of **adjectives** are identifiable on the basis of typical derivational suffixes. Many adjectives are also characterized by the fact that they inflect for the **comparative** and the **superlative**.

Some typical derivational suffixes of adjectives are:

-able (*-ible*)	: preferable, reasonable, visible
-ful	: beautiful, harmful, useful
-ic (*-ical*)	: economic(al), historic(al), allergic, nonsensical
-ish	: Danish, greenish, tallish
-ive	: abortive, massive, restive
-less	: endless, speechless, thoughtless
-like	: ladylike , manlike, warlike

Many adjectives take inflexional suffixes to form the comparative (*-er*) and the superlative degrees (*-est*). Comparison by inflexion is characteristic of monosyllabic adjectives:

bright – brighter – brightest
tall   – taller   – tallest

These suffixes are also found with many disyllabic adjectives, for example those that are stressed on the second syllable and those ending in *-er*, *-le*, *-ow* and *-y*:

mature – maturer – maturest
polite – politer – politest
sincere – sincerer – sincerest
clever – cleverer – cleverest
simple – simpler – simplest
narrow – narrower – narrowest
happy   – happier – happiest

A number of adjectives have irregular degrees of comparison. Among them are the following:

bad – worse   – worst
far – {farther / further} – {farthest / furthest}
good– better   – best

Adjectives that do not inflect for comparison are modified by *more* and *most*:

expensive   – more expensive   – most expensive
intelligent   – more intelligent – most intelligent
mysterious   – more mysterious – most mysterious

From a syntactic point of view we can distinguish between the attributive and the predicative use of adjectives. Most adjectives can be used attributively as well as predicatively. **Attributive adjectives** are constituents of the noun phrase and precede the noun phrase head (see subsection 6.1.2). **Predicative adjectives** function in the structure of the sentence as either subject attribute (see subsection 7.3.2.4) or object attribute (see subsection 7.3.2.5). Examples:

Attributive

a green door   that foolish idea
many witty remarks   John's beautiful wife

Attributive adjectives normally precede the noun phrase head. In some cases, however, they follow it (see subsection 6.1.3):

heir apparent
the persons responsible
somebody important
members willing to serve on the committee
students interested in Chomsky's theory of language

Predicative

subject attribute	*object attribute*
The door is green	We painted the door green
Your plan seems foolish	I consider your plan foolish
My tea is hot	I prefer my tea hot

Apart from the majority of adjectives which can be used both attributively and predicatively, there are adjectives that can only be used in one of these ways. Examples:

Attributive only

a mere girl	the latter solution
the upper storey	the principal reason
an utter fool	sheer nonsense
his sole argument	a silk scarf
the main cause	a metal tube
a former headmaster	his gold watch
a previous occasion	
the inner court	
the outer suburbs	

Predicative only

Most adjectives beginning with *a-* are used predicatively only. Examples:

asleep awake
alive   afraid
alike   ashamed
alone   aware

The class of predicative adjectives also includes the following:

loath (to)   dependent (on)
tantamount (to) intent (on)
flush (with)   prepared (to)
subject (to)

Note that some adjectives can be used both attributively and predicatively in one meaning, but are restricted to attributive use in another meaning:

Attributive and predicative:

an old book	– that book is old
a true story	– that story is true
a perfect solution	– that solution is perfect
real gold	– that gold is real
the right approach	– that approach is right

Attributive only:

An old friend	– *that friend is old
a true hero	– *that hero is true
a perfect fool	– *that fool is perfect
a real coward	– *that coward is real
the right man	– *that man is right

In other cases there is a semantic difference between the attributive and predicative use. Compare:

the present King – the King is present
his late wife   – his wife is late

2.2.3 *Adverbs*

Many **adverbs** can be identified on the basis of typical derivational suffixes. Some adverbs inflect for comparison.

Typical derivational suffixes for adverbs are:

-ly   : fully, intelligently, wisely
-ward(s) : afterwards, homewards, upward(s)
-wise   : clockwise, edgewise, lengthwise

Although *-ly* is the most productive of these suffixes, it should be borne in mind that not all words ending in *-ly* are adverbs. For instance, words like *beastly*, *friendly* and *lonely* belong to the class of adjectives.

Only a small number of adverbs inflect for comparison. The majority of these are identical in form with adjectives. Examples:

early – earlier   – earliest   soon – sooner – soonest
fast   – faster   – fastest   well   – better – best
hard   – harder   – hardest   badly – worse – worst
quick – quicker – quickest

Syntactically speaking we can distinguish two major functions of adverbs. They are either constituents of the sentence, in which case they function as adverbial (see section 7.4) or they modify the head in adjective and adverb phrases (see subsections 6.2.1 and 6.3.1).

When functioning as sentence constituents adverbs express such meanings as time, place, manner and degree. Examples:

The plane arrived yesterday
Peter is waiting outside
The soldiers were punished cruelly
He absolutely refused to come

They can also express the attitude of the speaker towards what he is saying, as in

Honestly, I don't have any money left
Unfortunately, they don't seem to understand

Finally, adverbs also have a linking function between one sentence and another:

John was ill. Nevertheless he turned up for the meeting
She is very kind-hearted. However, she is not a fool
The Joneses were very disappointed. So they left early

Adverbs can also be constituents of phrases. In this function they modify the head of an adjective or adverb phrase.

modifier of adjective phrase head	*modifier of adverb phrase head*
very interesting	hardly ever
exceptionally brave	fairly well
truly astonishing	rather quickly
really good	most optimistically
linguistically correct	almost always

2.2.4 *Verbs*

There are three derivational suffixes that are typical of the class of **verbs**:

-en	: broaden, darken, lengthen
-ify	: glorify, nullify, simplify
-ize/ise	: economize, nationalise, scandalize

Most English verbs can add four inflexional morphemes to the base:

1. $\{s_3\}$: 3rd person singular present tense indicative
2. $\{ed_1\}$: past tense
3. $\{ed_2\}$: *-ed* participle
4. $\{ing\}$: *-ing* participle

The various verbal forms and their uses are exemplified in Table 2.5 (on the terms imperative, subjunctive and indicative see section 3.5).

Table 2.5

Form	Use	Examples
BASE	1. infinitive 2. imperative 3. present tense indicative (except 3rd pers. sing.) 4. present tense subjunctive	1. He must *live* in London He used to *live* in London 2. *Live* now, pay later 3. I/you/we/they *live* in London 4. Long *live* the Queen!
BASE + $\{s_3\}$	3rd person singular present tense indicative	He *lives* in London
BASE + $\{ed_1\}$	past tense	He *lived* in London
BASE + $\{ed_2\}$	*-ed* participle	He has *lived* in London
BASE + $\{ing\}$	*-ing* participle	He is *living* in London

The present tense morpheme $\{s_3\}$ is regularly realized in three ways:

/s/ : after bases ending in voiceless sounds except sibilants, eg: walks, coughs, stops, prints

/z/ : after bases ending in voiced sounds except sibilants, eg: frees, mars, chews, purrs, snores, destroys, dries, pays, glows, rubs, begs, climbs, grins, settles, breathes

/ɪz/ : after bases ending in a sibilant:

/s/ : mixes, promises, tosses
/z/ : freezes, loses, seizes
/ʃ/ : fishes, rushes, washes
/ʒ/ : camouflages, rouges
/tʃ/ : catches, screeches, touches
/dʒ/ : alleges, budges, lodges

The past tense morpheme {ed₁} and the -*ed* participle morpheme {ed₂} of regular verbs are realized in three ways:

/t/ : after bases ending in voiceless sounds except /t/, eg:
    kissed, tripped, walked
/d/ : after bases ending in voiced sounds except /d/, eg:
    loathed, sinned, played
/ɪd/ : after bases ending in /t/ or /d/, eg:
    parted, rotted, loaded, scolded

The -*ing* participle morpheme {ing} is always realized as /ɪŋ/:

playing, nodding, kissing

The regular spelling of the present tense suffix {s₃} is -*s* or -*es*. The latter spelling is found in:

1. verbs ending in -*s*, -*z*, -*ch*, -*sh* and -*x*, eg:
   hisses, buzzes, catches, fishes, taxes
2. verbs ending in a consonant symbol + -*o*, eg:
   echoes, goes, vetoes. Note the pronunciation of *does* /dʌz/
3. verbs ending in a consonant symbol + -*y* (*y* changes into *i*), eg:
   cries, fancies, tries

The regular spelling of the past tense and -*ed* participle suffixes {ed₁} and {ed₂} is -*ed* or -*d*. The latter spelling is found when the verb ends in mute -*e*, eg: baked, loved, moved.

In four cases the spelling of the base is affected before the ending -*ed*:

1. in verbs ending in a consonant symbol + -*y* (where *y* changes into *i*), eg:
   denied, fancied, pitied, tried;
2. in verbs ending in a consonant symbol preceded by a single vowel symbol the final consonant symbol is doubled if the verb is monosyllabic or ends in a stressed syllable, eg:
   hugged, nodded, rubbed, stopped, admitted, occurred, preferred, regretted.
   Note the following exceptions to this rule: humbugged, handicapped, kidnapped, worshipped;
3. in verbs ending in -*l*, preceded by a single vowel symbol, *l* is doubled:
   cancelled, quarrelled, rebelled, signalled, travelled;
4. final -*c* is changed into -*ck*: bivouacked, picnicked, trafficked.

In three verbs final -*y* is changed into *i* before the ending -*d*:

lay – laid,   pay – paid,   say – said /sed/

The spelling of the *-ing* participle suffix is always *ing*. Before this ending the base undergoes the spelling changes mentioned under 2, 3 and 4 above in connection with the past tense and *-ed* participle suffixes. Hence we find:

- doubling of final consonant – nodding, stopping, admitting, regretting, worshipping
- doubling of final *-l* – cancelling, quarrelling, travelling
- *c → ck* – picnicking, trafficking

In addition, the spelling of the base is affected in the following cases:

1. mute *-e* is dropped, eg:
   changing, having, taking
   Exceptions: age – ageing,   dye – dyeing,   hoe – hoeing, singe – singeing
2. *-ie* changes into *y*, eg:
   dying, lying, tying, vying

English has well over 200 irregular verbs. An irregular verb forms its past tense or *-ed* participle (or both) in other ways than those described above for regular verbs. There are four possibilities, as illustrated in Table 2.6.

Table 2.6

	Base	Base + {ed$_1$}	Base + {ed$_2$}
All three forms identical, eg:	burst	burst	burst
	cast	cast	cast
	cost	cost	cost
	cut	cut	cut
	hit	hit	hit
	put	put	put
	set	set	set
All three forms different, eg:	begin	began	begun
	choose	chose	chosen
	do	did	done
	drink	drank	drunk
	go	went	gone
	lie	lay	lain
	swim	swam	swum
	wear	wore	worn
{ed$_1$} = {ed$_2$}, eg:	bring	brought	brought
	find	found	found
	hang	hung	hung
	keep	kept	kept
	lead	led	led
	sit	sat	sat
	teach	taught	taught
	win	won	won
	build	built	built
Base = {ed$_2$}	come	came	come
	run	ran	run

Classes of verbs

Within the class of verbs two subclasses can be distinguished: **auxiliary verbs** and **lexical verbs**. The former constitute a closed class, the latter an open class.

There are four major differences between lexical verbs and auxiliary verbs:

1. Lexical verbs require periphrastic *do* in negative sentences with *not*. Auxiliaries can co-occur with *not* and can have special contracted negative forms. Compare:

   Frank likes hamburgers   – *Frank likes not hamburgers
        Frank does not like hamburgers
   He can come tomorrow   – He cannot (can't) come tomorrow

2. Lexical verbs require periphrastic *do* in yes/no questions, in *WH*-questions where the *WH*-item is not the subject and in sentences opening with a negative adverbial. Auxiliaries can come before the subject. Compare:

   Mary plays the piano   – *Plays Mary the piano?
        Does Mary play the piano?
   Mary can play the piano   – Can Mary play the piano?
   Frank leaves tomorrow   – *When leaves Frank?
        When does Frank leave?
   Frank is leaving tomorrow   – When is Frank leaving?
   A doctor seldom visits all his   – *Seldom a doctor visits all his
        patients   patients
        Seldom does a doctor visit all
        his patients
   A doctor can seldom visit all   – Seldom can a doctor visit all
        his patients   his patients

3. Lexical verbs cannot be used in 'code'. Compare:

   Should I see a doctor? Yes, you should see a doctor
                       Yes, you should
   You can do it and I can do it
   You can do it and so can I
   Do your students love linguistics? *Yes, they love linguistics
                                      Yes, they do
   John writes and Peter writes
   *John writes and so writes Peter
   John writes and so does Peter

   The first two examples show that, instead of repeating the auxiliary verb together with the lexical verb (and its complement), it is possible to repeat the auxiliary verb only. The auxiliary in such sentences is said to be used in 'code', the key to the code being provided by the preceding context. The last two examples show that lexical verbs (and their complement, if any) must be 'picked up' by a form of *do*.

4. Lexical verbs cannot be used emphatically to express a contrast, but require emphatic *do*. Auxiliaries, on the other hand, can be used emphatically. Compare:

Your son did not see her – *Yes, he SAW her
                            Yes, he DID see her
Your son has not seen her– Yes, he HAS seen her

A number of verbs (all of which are followed by *to*- infinitives), such as *tend to, happen to, fail to, seem to, appear to, turn out to, be to, have to,* and *be going to*, are sometimes treated as constituting a class (the so-called semi-auxiliaries) intermediate between auxiliary verbs and lexical verbs. We shall look upon them as lexical verbs.

Auxiliary verbs

As a rule an auxiliary verb cannot stand on its own. It must be followed by a lexical verb, except in cases where the lexical verb (sometimes with other sentence constituents) is understood:

Can Harry come? Yes, he can (come)
Will Mary meet us at the station? Yes, she will (meet us at the station)

Auxiliary verbs (or 'helping verbs') fall into two classes: **modal auxiliaries** and **primary auxiliaries**. There are two important differences between modal auxiliaries and primary auxiliaries. The former are always finite and invariably occur as the first element of the verb phrase. The primary auxiliaries *have* and *be* have finite as well as non-finite forms (see section 3.5) and may occur in initial as well as in medial position in the verb phrase. The primary auxiliary *do* always occurs initially, is invariably finite and does not generally co-occur with other auxiliaries. Compare:

finite/initial	*non-finite/medial*	*lexical verb*
may	—	write
may	have	written
may	be	writing
may	be	written
has	been	writing
is	being	written
does	—	write

Modal auxiliaries

The class of modal auxiliaries comprises the following items: *can, may, must, shall* and *will*. In English modal auxiliaries are mutually exclusive. Consider:

*I shall can come
*He will must do it
*It must can be done
*He will not may go out

Dare, *need*, *ought (to)* and *used (to)* are marginal members of this class of auxiliaries because of the following reasons:

1. *dare* and *need* can be used both as auxiliaries and as lexical verbs:

LV	: He dares to ask me that!	LV	: He needs to be careful
Aux	: He daren't ask me that	Aux	: He needn't be careful
LV/Aux	: He doesn't dare (to) ask me that	LV	: He doesn't need to be careful
Aux	: Dare he ask me that?	Aux	: Need he be careful?
LV/Aux	: Does he dare (to) ask me that?	LV	: Does he need to be careful?

2. Unlike the other auxiliaries *ought* and *used* are followed by a *to*-infinitive. In addition *used* may co-occur with *do* in negative and interrogative sentences:

He usedn't to drive a car   He didn't use(d) to drive a car
Used he to drive a car?   Did he use(d) to drive a car?

Primary auxiliaries

English has three primary auxiliaries: *do*, *have* and *be*.

Do differs from *have* and *be* in that it usually co-occurs with lexical verbs only. This means that verb phrases with *do* contain only two verb forms, since verb phrases cannot have more than one lexical verb:

Do come, John!
Do you believe him?
You don't believe him

Have and *be* co-occur not only with lexical verbs but also with modal auxiliaries; they always follow the latter:

He may have escaped
You will be punished
You should be preparing your lecture

Have and *be* also co-occur with each other; *have* always precedes *be*:

He has been sent abroad
The children have been messing about in the library
The prisoners have been being interrogated by the police

Do

Do is used as an **auxiliary of periphrasis** and of **emphasis**. In the former function it occurs in negative sentences with *not*, in interrogative sentences (with the exception of *WH-* questions opening with the subject) and in declarative sentences opening with a negative adverbial. Examples:

negative: He does not realize what he is doing
                            I did not see John last night

| interrogative: | Do you think you can come? |
| | Who did he see? (cf Who saw him?) |

| negative/interrogative: | Why doesn't he leave tonight? |
| | Didn't you get up in time? |

| negative adverbial: | Only then did he realize his position |
| | Rarely did they leave the house |

Emphatic *do* can be used in declarative sentences, in *WH-* questions opening with the subject and in imperative sentences. Examples:

| declarative: | He DOES know what he is talking about |
| | I DID lock the door, you know |

| *WH-* questions opening with the subject: | But who DOES understand him? |
| | What then DID cause the explosion? |

| imperative: | DO try and be careful! |
| | DO be sensible! |

Note that emphatic forms of periphrastic *do* also occur in sentences like the following in which *do* is required as an auxiliary anyway:

negative:	But he DOESN'T know the answer!
interrogative:	But DOES he know the answer?
	But who DOESN'T know the answer?

| negative/interrogative: | But DOESN'T he know the answer? |

Periphrastic and emphatic *do* do not co-occur with *be* except in negative and emphatic imperatives. Cf:

 *He doesn't be careful
 *He does be careful
 Don't be a fool!
 Don't be tempted!
 Don't be saying things like that!
 Do be careful!

Periphrastic do is optional in negative and interrogative sentences containing the verb *have* meaning 'possess', eg:

 He hasn't any money – He doesn't have any money
 Has she any children? – Does she have any children?

The use of periphrastic *do* is as a rule preferred in the past tense. Sentences like *He didn't have any money* and *Did he have any children?* are more common than *He hadn't any money* and *Had he any children?*
The various uses and forms of the auxiliary *do* are listed in Table 2.7.

Table 2.7

Use		Forms
Periphrastic *do* in —	┌ negative sentences with *not* ├ interrogative sentences (except *WH-* questions │ opening with the subject) └ sentences opening with a negative adverbial	}do, does, did
Emphatic *do* in —	┌ declarative sentences ├ *WH-* questions opening with the subject └ imperative sentences	}do, does, did

Apart from its use as an auxiliary there are two other uses of *do* (in both uses *do* has the full range of forms):

1. Lexical verb. Examples:
   He is doing a good job
   Does Jennifer do the household?

2. Pro-verb substituting for the verb phrase (often together with other elements of the sentence). In this function *do* may co-occur with *so* (see subsection 2.2.9.8), *that* and *it*. Examples:
   Who knows the answer? John does
   Peter knows the answer. So does John/So he does
   Who broke that vase? I think Mary did that
   Peter promised to send me his new novel next week but I doubt if he will do it.

Have and Be

Have and *be* function as auxiliaries of aspect. *Have* is **auxiliary of the perfective aspect** when followed by the *-ed* participle of another verb. *Be* is **auxiliary of the progressive aspect** when it combines with the *-ing* participle of another verb. Examples:

He has written a new novel
He may have written a new novel
He is writing a new novel
He may be writing a new novel

The following examples illustrate co-occurrences of *have* and *be* as aspectual auxiliaries:

He has been writing a new novel
He may have been writing a new novel

Be is also used as **auxiliary of the passive voice** when followed by the *-ed* participle of a transitive (lexical) verb:

The theatre was built in 1970
The theatre may be built next year

The following examples illustrate co-occurrences of *be* as auxiliary of the passive voice with the aspectual auxiliaries *have* and *be*:

The theatre has already been built
The theatre is being built
The theatre has been being built for three years now

Both aspectual and passive *be* exhibit all finite and non-finite forms. So does aspectual *have* with the exception of the *-ed* participle.

Apart from their use as auxiliaries *have* and *be* also occur as lexical verbs. Examples:

Did you have a good time?
He has two children
John's wife is a good cook
The meeting is at six

The above classification of auxiliary verbs is summarized in Table 2.8.

Table 2.8

AUXILIARIES	Modal auxiliaries:		CAN, MAY, MUST, SHALL, WILL DARE, NEED, OUGHT (TO), USED (TO)
	Primary Auxiliaries	DO ⎰	auxiliary of periphrasis
		⎱	auxiliary of emphasis
		HAVE:	auxiliary of the perfective aspect
		BE ⎰	auxiliary of the progressive aspect
		⎱	auxiliary of the passive voice

Lexical verbs

Lexical verbs constitute the principal part of the verb phrase. They can be accompanied by auxiliaries, but they can also occur in verb phrases that do not contain any other verbal forms. Cf:

John may   move next week
John may be moving next week
John   moved last week

There are two ways of classifying lexical verbs. The first is based on complementation, the second involves the distinction between one-word and multi-word verbs.

Complement verbs and intransitive verbs

A classification based on complementation depends on whether or not the lexical verb in a sentence can occur on its own (ie without a complement) or is obligatorily followed by words that complement its meaning. The two major classes that can be set up in this way are those of verbs that do not require a complement (**intransitive verbs**) and verbs that do (**complement verbs**). The following examples contain intransitive verbs:

Dogs bark	The leaves are falling
The baby is sleeping	My head aches
The brooch had disappeared	The judge yawned

The class of complement verbs consists of two subclasses: **transitive** complement verbs and **non-transitive** complement verbs. Some transitive complement verbs require only a direct object (DO; see subsection 7.3.2.1). Others are, in addition, accompanied by another complement, ie by an indirect object (IO; see subsection 7.3.2.2), a benefactive object (BO; see subsection 7.3.2.3), an object attribute (OA; see subsection 7.3.2.5) or a predicator complement (PC; see subsection 7.3.2.6). The four classes of transitive verbs thus distinguished are:

1. **monotransitive verbs** (DO only):
   The farmer kicked the horse
2. **ditransitive verbs** (IO + DO/BO + DO):
   He gave her a book
   He called her a taxi
3. **complex transitive verbs** (DO + OA):
   They find him a bore
4. **transitive PC verbs** (DO + PC):
   That play reminds me of Shakespeare

Non-transitive complement verbs comprise two sub-classes: copulas (or linking verbs), ie verbs that are followed by a subject attribute (SA; see subsection 7.3.2.4) and verbs that are followed by a predicator complement without an accompanying direct object (see subsection 7.3.2.6, exs. 190-196):

1. **copulas** (SA):
   John is a teacher
   Mary fell ill
2. **non-transitive PC verbs** (PC):
   He resembles his father
   This book belongs to Jane

The above classification of lexical verbs is summarized in Table 2.9.

Table 2.9

LEXICAL VERBS	Complement verbs	Transitive complement verbs	Monotransitive verbs Ditransitive verbs Complex transitive verbs Transitive PC verbs	(DO only) (IO + DO or BO + DO) (DO + OA) (DO + PC)
		Non-transitive complement verbs	Copulas Non-transitive PC verbs	(SA) (PC only)
	Intransitive verbs:		no complement	

One-word verbs and multi-word verbs

One-word verbs consist of one single lexical item, **multi-word verbs** of at least two. Multi-word verbs fall into four subclasses:

1. phrasal verbs
2. prepositional verbs
3. phrasal-prepositional verbs
4. Verb + Noun + Preposition idioms

Examples:

One-word verbs:

become   fall   lack   read
convince give   make swim

Multi-word verbs:

| Phrasal verbs: | bring about | catch on | make up | stand out |
| | call up | draw up | set out | step down |

| Prepositional verbs: | account for | concentrate on | insist on | look for |
| | allow for | enlarge on | listen to | part with |

| Phrasal-prepositional verbs: | catch up with | feel up to | go in for | look up to |
| | come down to | get on with | lash out at | put down to |

Verb + Noun + Preposition idioms:	catch sight of	give way to	lay claim to
	get hold of	keep track of	lose touch with
	set fire to	take leave of	

Phrasal verbs are combinations of a verb and a member of a closed set of adverbs: *about, across, along, around, aside, away. back, by, down, forth, in, off, on, out, over, up.*

Phrasal verbs are either complement verbs (a) or intransitive verbs (b):

(a) His father drew up a new will
    Did you make up this story?
(b) John's new idea did not catch on
    We set out at dawn

Prepositional verbs are combinations of a verb and a preposition. They are usually monotransitive complement verbs, in other words the constituent that follows them functions as direct object:

How do you account for this phenomenon?
The speaker did not enlarge on this subject
Why did not you listen to his advice?
We are looking for an alternative solution

There are two major differences between phrasal and prepositional verbs:

1. As a rule the adverb in phrasal verbs is stressed. In prepositional verbs the stress falls on the verb, the preposition being unstressed. Compare:

    They have called úp all applicants for an interview
    It is better not to cáll on him
    Why don't you look úp the word in a dictionary?
    Just lóok at him!

2. In transitive phrasal verbs the adverb can generally occur both before and after the direct object constituent. Compare:

    Did you make up this story? – Did you make this story up?
    How do you account for this phenomenon? – *How do you account
                                                      this phenomenon for?

Note that the adverb in a phrasal verb must follow the direct object constituent if this is a pronoun:

    Did you give it up? – *Did you give up it?

Phrasal-prepositional verbs are combinations of a verb, an adverb and a preposition. The majority of them are non-transitive PC verbs. Examples:

    I am afraid I do not feel up to the job
    We do not get on with our neighbours
    Do you go in for squash?
    The police caught up with the speeding car near Marble Arch

In **Verb + Noun + Preposition idioms** the noun cannot be modified nor can it become the subject of a passive sentence. Consider:

    We caught sight of the plane
    *We caught sudden sight of the plane
    They kept track of all his movements
    *Track was kept of all his movements

For these reasons we look upon such idioms as indivisible units having the function of predicator (see subsection 8.3.1) in the structure of the sentence. These multi-word verbs are always monotransitive.

Other Verb + Noun + Preposition sequences resemble the *catch sight of* type illustrated above. Some examples are:

make allowance for	put pressure on
make fun of	take advantage of
make use of	take care of
pay attention to	take notice of

These are similar to the *catch sight of* type in that they are monotransitive, that is the constituent that follows them can become the subject of a passive sentence:

    He was last caught sight of disappearing over the edge of the cliff
    His illness should have been made allowance for

They differ, however, from the *catch sight of* type in two respects: (a) the noun in the sequence can be modified and (b) the noun can function as the subject of a passive sentence:

(a) Jimmy has not taken proper care of his car
     We have paid considerable attention to your criticism
(b) Great pressure has been put on the Government to reduce taxation
     Hardly any notice was taken of what they were saying

2.2.5 *Prepositions*

Prepositions constitute a closed word class, and are formally invariable. We distinguish **simple** (one-word) and **complex** (multi-word) prepositions. Examples:

	Simple		*Complex*	
at	in	according to	in front of
before	of	as to	in spite of
between	on	because of	in terms of
by	since	by means of	on account of
despite	until	by virtue of	on behalf of
during	up	in accordance with	out of
from	with	in addition to	with regard to

2.2.6 *Conjunctions*

Like prepositions, **conjunctions** constitute a closed set of words which do not vary in form. On formal grounds conjunctions can be divided into two classes: **simple** and **complex**. Examples:

	Simple		*Complex*	
and	if	as if	in case
because	since	as long as	insofar as
before	that	as soon as	now that
but	while	as though	so that

On functional grounds we can distinguish between coordinating conjunctions (**coordinators**) and subordinating conjunctions (**subordinators**). Coordinators function as linkers between sentences, clauses and phrases. English has four coordinators: *and*, *but*, *or* and *for*. The coordinator *but* cannot link noun phrases, while *for* cannot link clauses and phrases. Examples:

and : Tom is staying in England and we are going to France
      We can only go if Mary looks after the children and Peter takes
         care of the dogs
      John and his colleagues have decided to resign

but : Susan is nice, but she is rather stubborn
      We gather that he is likeable but that he is also boring
      Veronica is a rather plain but very intelligent girl

or : Is John still married or has his wife divorced him?
Was he late because he had overslept or because he had missed his train?
Do you take your tea with lemon or with milk?

for : Alex cannot come to the wedding, for his father died last night

Coordination (see subsection 4.3.1) often involves 'understood' elements:

I saw Jim and (I saw) Catherine
The book is interesting but (the book is) expensive
Is she married or (is she) single?

This is impossible after *for*. Compare:

Harry cannot come for he is ill
*Harry cannot come for is ill

Sentences like the above can be described as cases of phrasal or of sentential coordination, depending on whether or not we want to account syntactically for the understood elements. The following sentences, however, can only be regarded as containing instances of phrasal coordination:

This beautiful car and example of British craftsmanship is yours at the price of £16,000
John's friend and lifelong companion died in France last week
The poet and painter Hugh Windmill is now having an exhibition at the Tate Gallery

Coordinators also sometimes link words. Compare:

Word coordination:
The man was waving a black and white flag
The jockey wore a red and white cap
The Stars and Stripes was flying from a flagpole in the garden of the White House

Phrasal coordination:
The students were waving black flags and white ones
The jockey wore a red cap and a white shirt
How many stars and stripes are there on the American flag?

Neither and *nor* are marginal coordinators, since they do not only occur by themselves but can be preceded by *and* or *but*:

Dick did not apply for his job, (and) nor did Tom
Jaguars are not particularly cheap, (but) neither are Bentleys

And, but, nor and *or* also function as the second members of so-called **correlative pairs**: *both . . . and, not only . . . but (also), neither . . . nor* and *either . . . or.*

Examples:

> Both Wordsworth and Coleridge lived in the Lake District
> He not only invited her to dinner but also took her to a nightclub
> I am neither enthusiastic nor disappointed
> We shall either leave early or stay until the end

Subordinators introduce subclauses, that is clauses functioning as consti-tuents of sentences or phrases. The subordinators in the following examples introduce clauses that function as sentence constituents:

> That she is in love is obvious
> I do not know whether he is in
> Do you mind if I smoke?
> I cannot come since my mother is ill
> Let us wait in case he turns up
> Why do not you talk to him as I did?
> Though the situation is alarming, he will not commit suicide

Subordinators also introduce clauses that function as constituents of noun phrases, adjective phrases and adverb phrases:

> the day before he died
> the hope that he would recover
> easier than we expected
> as unfriendly as he used to be
> more bravely than he had ever behaved before
> as effectively as we had hoped

2.2.7 Articles

English has two types of article, which function exclusively as constituents of the noun phrase. The **definite article** is spelled *the*, the **indefinite article** is spelled *a* (before consonants) or *an* (before vowels). The pronunciation depends on the initial sound of the following word or on whether the article is stressed or unstressed (see Table 2.10).

Table 2.10

Article	Spelling	Pronunciation	
		Unstressed	Stressed
Definite	the	/ðə/ (before consonants) /ðɪ/ (before vowels)	/ði/
Indefinite	a (before consonants)	/ə/	/eɪ/
	an (before vowels)	/ən/	/æn/

Examples:

/ðə/ : the man, the use
/ðɪ/ : the error, the hour
/ði/ : John is *the* man for the job
/ə/   : a book, a unit
/ən/ : an uncle, an honour
/eɪ/ : I said '*a* man', not '*the* man'
/æn/ : He understood '*an* option', not '*the* option'

Note that the indefinite article is *a* or *an* before some words spelled with initial *h*, depending on whether the *h* is pronounced or not: *a(n) hotel, a(n) historical event.*

2.2.8 Numerals

We distinguish two sets of **numerals**: **cardinal numbers** and **ordinal numbers.**

Cardinal numbers

0 nought, zero		20 twenty	
1 one		21 twenty-one	
2 two		22 twenty-two	
3 three	13 thirteen	23 twenty-three	30 thirty
4 four	14 fourteen	24 twenty-four	40 forty
5 five	15 fifteen	25 twenty-five	50 fifty
6 six	16 sixteen	26 twenty-six	60 sixty
7 seven	17 seventeen	27 twenty-seven	70 seventy
8 eight	18 eighteen	28 twenty-eight	80 eighty
9 nine	19 nineteen	29 twenty-nine	90 ninety
10 ten			
11 eleven			
12 twelve			

100	one hundred, a hundred
101	one hundred and one, etc
200	two hundred, etc
1,000	one thousand, a thousand
1,001	one thousand and one, etc
1,100	one thousand and one hundred, eleven hundred, etc
2,000	two thousand, etc
10,000	ten thousand, etc
100,000	one hundred thousand, a hundred thousand, etc
1,000,000	one million, a million, etc

Note that *hundred, thousand* and *million* may be preceded not only by *one*, but also by *a*. They can also be pluralized, as in

hundreds of thousands of victims
millions of locusts

Ordinal numbers

1st	first	13th	thirteenth, etc
2nd	second	20th	twentieth
3rd	third	21st	twenty-first
4th	fourth	22nd	twenty-second
5th	fifth	23rd	twenty-third, etc
6th	sixth	30th	thirtieth, etc
7th	seventh	100th	(one) hundredth, etc
8th	eighth	101st	(one) hundred and first, etc
9th	ninth	1,000th	(one) thousandth
10th	tenth	1,001st	(one) thousand and first, etc
11th	eleventh	100,000th	(one) hundred thousandth, etc
12th	twelfth	1,000,000th	(one) millionth, etc

Both cardinal and ordinal numbers function in the structure of the noun phrase or as constituents of the sentence:

> Forty is an interesting age
> There were forty guests at Jim's party
> Forty of the passengers were killed
> Did your horse come first?
> The first concert starts at eight
> He was the first to arrive

Cardinal numbers can be modified by adverbs such as *about*, *almost*, *approximately*, *nearly*, *over*, etc:

> There were about 200 students
> Mr McPherson is over 70 years of age

2.2.9 *Pronouns*

Pronouns are usually treated as forming one word class with several subclasses. We shall follow this classification, although both syntactically, morphologically and semantically it is hard to find properties that all pronouns share. We distinguish the following subclasses of pronouns, all of which are closed classes:

Personal pronouns	Relative pronouns
-*self* pronouns	Interrogative pronouns
Demonstrative pronouns	Reciprocal pronouns
Possessive pronouns	*So* and *one*

2.2.9.1 Personal pronouns

As Table 2.11 shows, the **personal pronouns** are marked for **person** (1st person, 2nd person and 3rd person) and also (with the exception of *you* and *it*) for **case** (subjective case and objective case) and **number** (singular and plural). The third person singular personal pronouns are also marked for **gender** (masculine, feminine and neuter).

Table 2.11

Person	Case	Number	
		singular	plural
1st person	subjective	*I*	*we*
	objective	*me*	*us*
2nd person	subjective	*you*	
	objective		
3rd person	subjective	masculine : *he* feminine : *she* neuter : *it*	*they*
	objective	masculine : *him* feminine : *her* neuter : *it*	*them*

The personal pronouns may be looked upon as noun phrases of the simplest possible structure, which, as a rule, allow neither premodification nor postmodification. They occur in the **subjective case** when functioning as the subject of a sentence, in the **objective case** in all other functions. Both cases are found when the pronoun functions as subject attribute (see subsection 7.3.2.4), the subjective case being more formal. Examples:

I am your new secretary
She gave them to me
It is I/me
Would you mind shutting that window? Who, me?

The third person singular personal pronouns *he/him*, *she/her* and *it* show gender distinctions. *He* and *him* are used to refer to nouns with male referents, *she* and *her* to refer to nouns with female referents and *it* to refer to inanimate nouns. Note that names of countries and ships can be referred to by both *she/her* and *it*.

2.2.9.2 *Self*-pronouns

The *self*-**pronouns** are marked for person and number, but not for case. In addition the third person singular *self*-pronouns are marked for gender (see Table 2.12). The *self*-pronoun corresponding to the pronoun *one* is *oneself*, as in

One should never compromise oneself in this way

Self-pronouns can be used reflexively, in apposition, in coordinated phrases and after the words *as*, *but*, *except* and *like*. When reflexive they are either emphatic or non-emphatic.

Table 2.12

Person	Number	
	singular	plural
1st person	*myself*	*ourselves*
2nd person	*yourself*	*yourselves*
3rd person	masculine : *himself* feminine : *herself* neuter : *itself*	*themselves*

Reflexive *self*-pronouns replace coreferential noun phrases and usually function as constituents of the sentence:

I watched myself in the mirror
That man is not himself
Are you going to give yourself a treat?

Reflexive *self*-pronouns also occur in prepositional phrases:

John is very proud of himself
Why don't you speak for yourself?
They are obviously very pleased with themselves

Note that after prepositions denoting place the objective case of the personal pronouns is used instead of the corresponding *self*-pronouns:

He had a pile of books in front of him
Meg looked behind her to see where her dog was
I wrapped the blanket around me

When the preposition is used in a non-literal sense, however, the *self*-pronoun is sometimes obligatory, as in

The man was beside himself with anger

Self-pronouns are used in apposition to nouns and pronouns:

Did you have lunch with the President himself?
The chairman himself abstained from voting
She herself is not to be blamed

Note the mobility of the *self*-pronoun when it is part of the subject of the sentence:

He himself was not there
He was not there himself

The use of *self*-pronouns in coordinated phrases is illustrated by the examples below, where they occur in free variation with personal pronouns:

John and myself (John and I) were the only visitors
For her brother and herself (for her brother and her) this must have been
  a terrifying experience

The invitation was addressed to the Joneses and ourselves (to the Joneses and us)

Finally, *self*-pronouns occur in free variation with personal pronouns after the words *as*, *but*, *except* and *like*:

She must be about the same age as yourself (as you)
No one but myself (but me) was worried
Everybody except ourselves (except us) seemed to be going
For a woman like yourself (like you) the future should look bright

2.2.9.3 Demonstrative pronouns

There are four **demonstrative pronouns** in English: *this* and *that* (singular), *these* and *those* (plural). *This/these* refer to what is near (spatially, temporally and psychologically), *that/those* to what is remote. Demonstrative pronouns function as constituents of the sentence or in the structure of the noun phrase. Examples:

Is this book yours?
This is John's book
I am seeing Dorothy this afternoon
When I came out of Harrods I saw this lovely girl
These are my friends
These photographs are the best
Was that what you had expected?
What do you think of that?
I don't like that man
Those were the days
Were those Mary's children?
We have all heard those stories before

Both *that* and *those* can be followed by relative clauses. The relative pronoun after *that* is *which* (this usage is fairly rare, *what* being more usual than *that which*). The relative pronoun after *those* is either *which* (non-personal reference) or *who* (personal reference). Examples:

That which used to be old-fashioned is now all the rage
    (What used to be old-fashioned . . .)
Did you read those which came in this morning?
John taught those who were only beginners

2.2.9.4 Possessive pronouns

Within the class of **possessive pronouns** we can distinguish the categories of person (1st person, 2nd person and 3rd person), number (except for the 2nd person) and gender (in the 3rd person singular only). There are two subclasses of possessive pronouns: those which function dependently, that is as determiners in the structure of the noun phrase (see section 3.2) and those which function independently, that is as heads of noun phrases. The various forms are listed in Table 2.13.

Table 2.13

Subclass	Person	Number	
		singular	plural
Dependent	1st person	*my*	*our*
	2nd person	*your*	
	3rd person	masculine : *his* feminine : *her* neuter : *its*	*their*
Independent	1st person	*mine*	*ours*
	2nd person	*yours*	
	3rd person	masculine : *his* feminine : *hers* neuter : -	*theirs*

Examples:
   Is this your present? What about mine?
   Some friends of ours live in France
   Their house is up for sale
   Are you sure this bag is hers?

2.2.9.5 Relative pronouns

The **relative pronouns** are *who, whose, whom, which* and *that*. They are used to introduce **relative clauses**, that is clauses normally functioning as postmodifiers in the structure of the noun phrase (see subsection 6.1.3). The relative pronoun *which* may have a noun phrase as well as a sentence as its antecedent. In the latter case we have a sentential relative clause, which does not function in the structure of a noun phrase. *That* differs from the other relative pronouns in introducing restrictive relative clauses only and also in having no case contrast (cf *who/whose/whom* and *which/whose*). The relative pronoun *whose* can only be used as a determiner, *which* can be used as a determiner as well as independently, *who, whom* and *that* are used independently only.

As Table 2.14 shows, the choice of relative pronoun depends on the reference of the antecedent as well as on the type of relative clause in which the pronoun occurs.

Table 2.14

Reference of the antecedent	Type of relative clause	
	Restrictive	Non-Restrictive
Personal	*who, whose, whom, that*	*who, whose, whom*
Non-personal	*which, whose, that*	*which, whose*
Sentence	—	*which*

Examples:

Restrictive relative clauses

Personal reference: The man who caused the accident escaped
People who live in glasshouses should not throw stones
Is he the boy whose bike was stolen?
The girl who(m) the police suspect was arrested last night
The man to whom you were talking (who(m) you were talking to) is our chairman
John is a man that knows about such things

Non-personal
reference: The situation in which he found himself was desperate
ICI is a company whose export figures are likely to improve next year
This is something that requires immediate attention
Any book that he writes is bound to sell well

Note that the relative pronoun in restrictive relative clauses can be left out unless it is the subject of the relative clause or is preceded by a preposition. Hence some of the above sentences have the following alternative forms:

The girl the police suspect was arrested last night
The man you were talking to is our chairman
The situation he found himself in was desperate
Any book he writes is bound to sell well

It should also be noted that the pronoun *that* is used instead of *which* when the antecedent is modified by a superlative or when the antecedent is *all*, *anything* and *everything*; *that* is used instead of *who* in the function of subject attribute:

This is the best film that was released last week
I was not convinced by anything that was said
Bill is not the optimist (that) he used to be

Non-restrictive relative clauses

Personal reference: My sister, who lives in New York, is coming over for Christmas

Two of my friends, whose wives have jobs, take the children to school in the morning

The proofs were read by Bill Frazer, to whom I am greatly indebted

His grandmother, who(m) I greatly admire, spends every winter in Spain

Non-personal reference:

These houses, which are owned by the Town Council, are going to be pulled down

The committee proposed two solutions, neither of which is acceptable

Why don't you fly KLM, whose service is said to be very good?

The ambulance arrived an hour later, by which time the boy had died

Sentential reference:

Christopher has pneumonia, which explains his absence

Graham is going to divorce his wife, which does not surprise me in the least

Suddenly Ophelia lost her wig, at which the audience burst out laughing

I had a flat tyre, as a result of which I missed my train

As appears from the above examples the objective case *whom* is obligatory when immediately preceded by a preposition. In all other cases *whom* can be replaced by *who*, the former being more formal.

The pronoun *what* can be used independently, that is without an antecedent. Semantically it is equivalent to 'that which'. *What* is used in sentences like the following:

What I don't understand is that he refused
This is what I have always wanted
Does this account for what he has done?
She does not believe what I say

The compound pronouns *whatever*, *whoever* and *whichever* are used in the same way:

You can do whatever you like
Whoever says that is wrong
The prize will go to whichever arrives first

Unlike *what*, the pronoun *who* is rarely used independently in the meaning of 'he/those who'. It occurs in standard expressions like

Who delays pays
Whom the Gods love die young

Normally, however, *who* is replaced by *The/a man (person) who . . .*, *anyone (anybody) who . . ., those who . . .* or by *whoever*:

The person who planted that bomb should be sent to prison
Anyone who witnessed the accident is asked to get in touch with the
    police
Those who want to take the exam should contact the secretary
Whoever makes such claims cannot be in his right mind

2.2.9.6 Interrogative pronouns

The **interrogative pronouns** are *who, whose, whom, what* and *which*. They are used to introduce direct *WH*-questions, as in

Who did that?
What is the matter with him?

as well as indirect *WH*-questions (after reporting verbs such as *ask*, *wonder*, etc), as in

He asked who did that
I wonder what is the matter with him

The interrogative pronouns *who* and *whom* are used independently only. *Whose, what* and *which* can function as determiners as well as independently. *Who, whose* and *whom* have personal reference only, *which* and *what* can have both personal and non-personal reference. The difference between *who* and *what* on the one hand and *which* on the other is that the use of the latter implies that a selection is made from a limited set. On the use of the objective case *whom* see relative *whom*.

Examples:
Who wrote *Sons and Lovers*?
Whose books are these?
Whose are these books?
Who(m) are you looking at?
To whom did you address the letter?
What man would follow such advice?
What is the square root of 144?
What dictionaries of English do you know?
Which dictionary would you recommend?
Which of them was published by Longman?
Which of your children plays the piano?

The word *ever* can be added as an emphatic element to the interrogative pronouns *who*, *what* and *which*. The resulting compounds are usually written in two words:

> Who ever told you that?
> What ever made you change your mind?
> Which ever should we vote for, Bill or John?

2.2.9.7 Reciprocal pronouns

The **reciprocal pronouns** are *each other* and *one another*. They are used independently (but not in the function of subject) in sentences with plural or coordinated subjects. *One another* is sometimes preferred to *each other* when reference is made to more than two. Both pronouns can occur in the genitive. Examples:

> Margaret and Sandy accuse each other of disloyalty
> My sisters have never written to each other since their marriage
> The children were admiring one another's Christmas presents

2.2.9.8 *So* and *one*

Since these words are difficult to classify, they are given separate treatment. *So* is mainly used:

1. As a substitute for a *that*-clause:

> Do you think he is going to marry her?
> I think so   John told me so
> I suppose so   So they say
> I hope so   So I was given to understand
> I'm afraid so So I hear
> It seems so

2. Together with the verb *do*, the combination *do so* substituting for the verb phrase and other constituents (if any):

> The manager told him to lock the safe but he forgot to do so
> I had hoped she would give me a present on my birthday and she did so
> The doctor advised her to go on a diet and she must have done so

Verb phrases containing a verb of bodily sensation or a verb of involuntary perception or cognition are usually replaced by *do* rather than *do so*. Compare:

> Agnes felt very sick.   I know she did
>   *I know she did so
> I suddenly smelled gas.   I did, too
>   *I did so, too
> He understands my problems.   Yes, he does.
>   *Yes, he does so

3. In sentence-initial position, followed by *be, have, do* or a modal auxiliary:

> John is a bachelor and so is his brother
> Our neighbours are going off tomorrow. So are we
> England was beaten but so was Holland
> Jennifer's father has a cottage in France. So has mine
> I have told him not to do it. So has John
> Phil spends all his money on horses and so does his son
> Jill should work a bit harder. So should you

Note that in the above examples the same thing is said about different subjects. If the same subject is involved there is no inversion. Compare:

> John is wearing new spectacles. So he (ie John) is
> So is Peter
> Peter works hard   So he (ie Peter) does
> So does Jane

One is not only used as a cardinal number, but also as:

1. A substitute word. In this function *one* is either a substitute for an indefinite noun phrase, as in

> Could you lend me a bike? I haven't got one
> I'm going to buy a record player. I thought you had one

or a substitute for a noun phrase head, in which case it must be preceded and/or followed by a modifying word, phrase or clause:

> Which girl do you mean? The one in the blue jeans
> This book is cheap but I'd rather have that one
> John reviews books but not the ones I'm interested in
> If you are going to buy a car, why don't you buy a small one?

In formal style *that* and *those* can be used instead of *the one* and *the ones*:

> This camera is better than that (the one) you bought
> I prefer these skis to those (the ones) you borrowed from Henry

Note that *one* cannot be used as a substitute for a mass noun. In that function the only possible pro-form is *that*:

> The cheapest gas is that from Holland
> The President's dishonesty is worse than that of his Ministers

Note also that *one* is not used after numerals, after a genitive and after the word *own*:

> We've got three children and the Johnsons have got two
> This car is Jack's
> Is this house your own?

2. A word referring to people in general, including the speaker or writer:

> One cannot deal with such problems on one's own
> One should never pity oneself too much
> He always gives one the impression that he is faking

2.2.10 *Quantifiers*

Quantifiers constitute a closed word-class, which can be divided into three subclasses:

1. Quantifiers which can only function as the head of a noun phrase:

someone	anyone	everyone	no one	none
somebody	anybody	everybody	nobody	
something	anything	everything	nothing	

   Examples:
   > Someone must have left the door open
   > We cannot invite just anybody
   > I seem to have forgotten everything
   > No one in his right mind would marry Jane
   > None of the girls has/have been invited

   The word *none* has pronominal characteristics in that it can serve as a substitute for plural count nouns and mass nouns:

   > John has got lots of friends but I've got none
   > We asked for petrol but they had none

2. Quantifiers which can function both as the head of a noun phrase and as determiner. To this subclass belong:

some	much } more, most
any	many }
each	little, less, least
all	few, fewer, fewest
both	enough
either	several
neither	

   Examples:
   > Some of the boys are orphans
   > Each student should have a medical examination
   > I rang my parents but both were out
   > Much of what he said is irrelevant
   > So far I have discovered few mistakes
   > We've got enough problems already

3. Quantifiers that function as determiner only. To this subclass belong *every* and *no*:

   > Every politician is responsible for his own constituency
   > He has no money and no prospects

2.2.11 *Interjections*

This word class consists of items that have no referring function and are only used to express emotions such as surprise, disgust, joy, pleasure, pain, etc.

Examples:

ah	blimey	hey	ouch /aʊtʃ/	yippee
aha	damn	oh	tut /ɪ, t ʌ t/	wow
blast	eh /eɪ/	oho	ugh /ʌx/	

Examples:

Aha, is that how it works?
Damn, I've dropped that glass!
Let's have a cup of coffee, eh?
Ugh, what a nasty taste!
Wow, isn't she a beauty?

3. The phrase

3.1 Introductory

Apart from the morpheme and the word there are two more major units of grammatical description: the phrase and the sentence or clause (on the distinction between 'sentence' and 'clause' see Chapter 4). The main difference between these two units is that a **phrase** is a constituent which can be identified on the basis of the word class membership of at least one of its constituent words, whereas a **sentence** (or **clause**) is identifiable on the basis of the relations holding among its immediate constituents.

The following phrases can be distinguished: **noun phrase, adjective phrase, adverb phrase**, **verb phrase** and **prepositional phrase**. A phrase can be identified on the basis of the word class membership of its most important constituent; thus a noun phrase is a phrase which has a noun as its most important constituent, an adjective phrase is a phrase whose principal element is an adjective, etc. However, the factors which determine which of the words of a phrase constitutes its principal part are not the same for all five phrase types. In three types, the noun phrase, the adjective phrase and the adverb phrase, the dominant element is that which can replace the whole phrase without affecting the structure of the sentence, as in the examples below:

Full phrase:	*Replaceable by:*	*Type of phrase:*
(1) We like *medieval music*	We like *music*	noun phrase
(2) *New books on linguistics* are very expensive	*Books* are very expensive	noun phrase
(3) John is *very worried about his youngest son*	John is *worried*	adjective phrase
(4) It was *so cold that my fingers were numb*	It was *cold*	adjective phrase
(5) She drives *much more carefully than her husband*	She drives *carefully*	adverb phrase
(6) He spoke *too hesitatingly to be convincing*	He spoke *hesitatingly*	adverb phrase

Following traditional nomenclature, we call the element that gives its name to a noun phrase, adjective phrase or adverb phrase, the **head** of the phrase. The other elements in the phrase stand, as the examples show, in a relation of dependency on, or subordination to, the head.

A fourth type of phrase, the verb phrase, is also characterized by a relation of subordination holding between the less important elements and the dominant element in the phrase. It differs, however, from the three phrases discussed above in that the dominance of the essential element mainly derives from semantic considerations and is only indirectly based on syntactic facts. In other words, the dominant member of a verb phrase cannot replace the whole phrase without causing serious harm to syntactic structure. Consider:

John *has been killed* by Bill—John *killed* by Bill

It is clear that, although from a semantic point of view *killed* is the dominant member in the phrase *has been killed*, it cannot replace the entire phrase. Phrases like *has been killed* are called verb phrases since they are exclusively made up of verbs. This holds without exception for every verb phrase.

Prepositional phrases are different from noun, adjective and adverb phrases, in that the element that gives its name to the phrase cannot be called its head since it cannot replace the whole phrase. Consider:

John darted *from the room*—*John darted *from*

It is obvious that the prepositional phrase is also different from the verb phrase in that only one of its constituents is a preposition, whereas in a verb phrase all the constituents are verbs.

The prepositional phrase differs from all other phrase types in the relation holding between the preposition and the other constituent of the phrase. This relation is not one of subordination but one of government. In a prepositional phrase, the preposition can be said to govern the other constituent of the phrase. In other languages this government relation is often more clearly manifested than it is in English. In a language like German, for instance, the preposition imposes a particular case on the constituent that it governs. In English this is only apparent when the preposition is followed by pronouns that show a distinction between subjective case and objective case. The preposition imposes the objective case on such pronouns:

Are you talking *to me*?
John is coming *with us*
For whom did you buy it?

The global characteristics of phrases that we have discussed so far, are summarized in Table 3.1. Each phrase is discussed individually in more detail in sections 3.2–3.6.

3.2 The noun phrase

As we have seen in the previous section, it is characteristic of a noun phrase that it has a dominant member (the head) which can replace the entire phrase; a characteristic that the noun phrase shares with the adjective phrase and the adverb phrase. At least as characteristic is a function in its internal structure that sets it apart from adjective and adverb phrases: the

Table 3.1

Phrase type	Relation between dominant member and other constituents	Characteristics of dominant member
Noun phrase	subordination	can replace the whole phrase
Adjective phrase	subordination	can replace the whole phrase
Adverb phrase	subordination	can replace the whole phrase
Verb phrase	subordination	cannot replace the whole phrase; semantically most important element
Prepositional phrase	government	cannot replace the whole phrase; imposes objective case on other constituent

determiner function. The words italicized in the following example noun phrases realize this function:

(7) *That* tall black man in the corner
(8) *The* book that I need
(9) *My* best suit
(10) *Every* boy in my class who has read the article
(11) *Any* major problem you may experience
(12) *A* well-designed car
(13) *Another* marble

As the examples show the function of determiner is invariably the first function that is realized in the noun phrase. In (7), (9), (11) and (12), for example, it would be impossible to put the determiner item immediately in front of the noun. It is also typical of the determiner function that, unlike other functions in the noun phrase, it cannot be realized more than once. Thus, examples (14) and (15) are unacceptable:

(14) *Every the book
(15) *His a car

A final syntactic characteristic of the determiner function is that it can, in general, only be realized by members from a closed class (see subsection 6.1.1). From a semantic point of view, the determiner function can be said to determine the reference of the noun phrase—whether its referent is definite or indefinite, whether one or more referents are intended, etc.

Clearly, the heads of the example noun phrases (7)–(13) are *man, book, suit, boy, problem, car* and *marble* respectively. All the other constituents, which, like the determiners, are subordinated to these heads, are said to function as **modifier**. Three differences between determiners and modifiers are immediately obvious. In the first place modifiers can occur both before and after the heads of noun phrases. If they precede the head, they are called **premodifiers**, if they follow the head they are called **postmodifiers**. Thus we have premodifiers in examples (7), (9), (11) and (12); postmodifiers occur in (7), (8), (10) and (11). A second difference with determiners is that the modifier function may be realized more than once in a noun phrase. In (7), for example, we have two premodifiers, *tall* and *black*; in (10) we have two postmodifiers, viz. *in my class* and *who has read the article*. Moreover, in examples (7) and (11) we have combinations of premodifier and postmodifier. In section 6.1 we shall see that it is also possible for a modifier to be interrupted by the head of the noun phrase. In this case we speak of a **discontinuous modifier**. A final difference between determiners and modifiers is that whereas it is only under very restricted conditions that the determiner function is not realized in a noun phrase, the occurrence of a modifier is never essential for the internal structure of a noun phrase. In none of the examples above, for instance, could the determiner be left out without rendering the phrase unacceptable. All of the modifiers, however, could easily be omitted without affecting the acceptability of the noun phrases.

From a semantic point of view modifiers show such a large variety of relations to the head word that it is impossible to discuss these relations here. One important semantic distinction, however, may be mentioned, viz. that between descriptive and classifying modifiers. A **descriptive modifier** describes the referent of the noun phrase in terms of a particular quality of the referent, whereas a **classifying modifier** creates a subclass of the class denoted by the head of the noun phrase. The distinction is illustrated in the examples below; examples of descriptive modifiers are given in (16) and (17), while (18) and (19) exemplify classifying modifiers.

(16) his *pretty* wife   (18) a *polar* bear
(17) that *tall* boy   (19) a *criminal* court

The distinction between descriptive and classifying modifiers largely correlates with the syntactic fact that descriptive modifiers may themselves be premodified by intensifying words like *very* to indicate the degree to which the referent of the noun phrase possesses the quality denoted by the modifying adjective; classifying modifiers, on the other hand, do not admit of intensification. Compare:

(16) a. his *very pretty* wife   (18) a. *a very polar* bear
(17) a. that *very tall* boy   (19) a. *a very criminal* court

In summary, we can say that in the internal structure of the noun phrase, three functions can be distinguished: determiner, modifier and head. The function of modifier is an optional one which may be realized more than once, may occur both in front of the head and after it, and may even be 'interrupted' by the head. The function of determiner is, in the majority of cases, an obligatory one which can be realized only once, is positionally restricted to the initial slot in the noun phrase and is usually realized by items from a number of closed classes. The item realizing the function of head determines the category of the phrase and is therefore realized by a noun or pronoun (for some exceptions see section 6.1); the head is, without exception, an obligatory function.

Noun phrases can function both as immediate constituents of sentences and as immediate constituents of other phrases. Sentence functions that are typically realized by noun phrases are those of subject (cf section 8.2), direct object (cf subsection 8.3.2.1), indirect object (cf subsection 8.3.2.2), benefactive object (cf subsection 8.3.2.3), subject attribute (cf subsection 8.3.2.4) and object attribute (cf. subsection 8.3.2.5). Since the use of noun phrases in these functions is illustrated extensively in the sections referred to, we shall here give only one example of each (for sentence functions see Chapter 7):

(20) *His wife* failed her driving-test   : subject
(21) Shall we plant *some rose-bushes* in that
     corner?   : direct object
(22) They gave *their old colleague* an
     encyclopedia   : indirect object
(23) Will you call *Mr Deighton* a taxi?   : benefactive object
(24) Jimmy is *the best student of his class*   : subject attribute
(25) The Board consider this *a very grave error of*
     judgment   : object attribute

There are two sentence-functions that are less closely associated with the noun phrase, that of predicator complement (cf subsection 8.3.2.6) and that of adverbial (cf section 8.4):

(26) His performance holds *much promise*:   predicator complement
(27) He suddenly turned up *last week*   :   adverbial

From the above survey of sentence functions realized by noun phrases it follows that, with the exception of the predicator function (cf subsection 8.3.1), all constituents of sentences can be noun phrases.

As far as phrase-internal functions are concerned, the only phrase type in which the noun phrase functions as a typical immediate constituent, is the prepositional phrase. In prepositional phrases the noun phrase is the usual realization of the function prepositional complement (cf section 6.5).

Examples:

(28) within *the danger zone*
(29) opposite *the supermarket*
(30) in spite of *the measures that were taken*

Occasionally noun phrases are found to perform certain phrase-internal functions which are usually realized by other constituents than noun phrases. Since these functions are non-typical of the noun phrase, they are not or only cursorily discussed in Chapter 6, where the more usual realizations of phrase-internal functions are dealt with. For that reason they are briefly discussed and illustrated below (examples 31–52).

(a) Sometimes a noun phrase is found within another noun phrase, where it follows the head of that phrase in a function resembling that of postmodifier, for example:

(31) a city *the size of Amsterdam*
(32) an apparatus *the size of a washing-machine*
(33) two children *your age*
(34) a car *the colour of red cabbage*

The nouns that can function as head in such postmodifying noun phrases are limited in number. Moreover the determiner is always definite, as the examples show.

(b) In adjective and adverb phrases denoting measure (time, space, weight, etc) noun phrases may function as premodifiers:

Adjective phrases	*Adverb phrases*
(35) *a yard* long	(40) *years* ago
(36) *one year* old	(41) *some months* earlier
(37) *two pounds* heavier	(42) *two years* previously
(38) *four fathom* deep	(43) *several miles* faster
(39) *two fingers* thick	(44) *a week* later

The examples show that the adjective or adverb that is premodified refers to such concepts as space, time, velocity, weight, etc. The premodifying noun phrase must have a head denoting a unit by which these concepts can be 'measured'. The premodifying noun phrase may either not contain a determiner (40) or, if it does, the determiner function is realized by the indefinite article (35, 44), a numeral (36, 37, 38, 39, 42) or a quantifier (41, 43).

What makes the above examples adjective and adverb phrases with premodifying noun phrases, rather than noun phrases with an adjective or adverb in postmodification, is the fact that in each the whole phrase can be replaced by the adjective or adverb (cf 45a and 46a). In none of the examples can the noun phrase function as the dominant member (cf 45b and 46b):

(45)   This box is two pounds heavier than that
(46)   They had moved house some months earlier
(45) a.   This box is heavier than that
(46) a.   They had moved house earlier
(45) b.   *This box is two pounds than that
(46) b.   *They had moved house two months

(c) Noun phrases denoting time and distance may also be used in premodification to prepositional phrases:

(47) *three yards* behind me
(48) *two miles* down the road
(49) *a week* after his death
(50) *two hours* before his arrival

That in the above examples we are dealing with premodified prepositional phrases rather than with noun phrases postmodified by prepositional phrases, is apparent from the fact that in each case the whole
constituent can be replaced by the prepositional phrase, but not by the
noun phrase. Compare, for example:

(48) a. He lives two miles down the road
     b. He lives down the road
     c. *He lives two miles

In a similar way, noun phrases denoting measures of time can occur as
premodifiers of temporal subordinators:

(51) *a week* after he died
(52) *two hours* before he arrived

One type of phrase-like constituent has remained undiscussed so far,
viz. the **apposition**. We discuss it here because its component parts are
noun phrases. An apposition usually contains two noun phrases. Some
examples are:

(53) *Peg Gibson, my best friend,* runs a crèche in Neasden
(54) *John's father, a very rich man,* has bought him a flat in Kensington
(55) *His disease, cirrhosis of the liver,* is causing him a lot of distress
(56) *Fausto Coppi, the greatest cyclist the world has known,* was born in
     a small Italian village
(57) The committee has appointed *Derek Mateson, the present person-
     nel manager*

The general characteristics of appositions are the following:

(a) Usually, either of the two noun phrases can replace the whole
    constituent; thus by the side of (53) we can have:

    (53) a. *Peg Gibson* runs a crèche in Neasden
         b. *My best friend* runs a crèche in Neasden

    The relation between the two noun phrases is neither one of subordina-
    tion nor of agreement, but rather one of concatenation, that is the two
    noun phrases are of equal syntactic weight.

(b) In general, the order of the two noun phrases can be inverted without
    causing a change in meaning. An alternative form of (53) would
    therefore be:

    (53) c. *My best friend, Peg Gibson* runs a crèche in Neasden

(c) From a semantic point of view, the two noun phrases in an apposition
    are also equivalent, in that both noun phrases are referentially identi-
    cal. In sentence (53), for example, *Peg Gibson* and *My best friend* refer
    to one and the same person.

(d) Finally, from the fact that an apposition is *one* constituent, that either
    noun phrase can replace the constituent and that the two noun phrases

are identical in reference, it follows that the two noun phrases always realize one and the same function in the sentence. In examples (53–56) this is the subject function, in (57) it is the function of direct object.

3.3 The adjective phrase

Apart from the adjectival head we distinguish only one other function in the adjective phrase, that of modifier. Similarly to the modifier in the noun phrase, it is called premodifier when the constituent realizing this function precedes the head, postmodifier when this constituent follows it. The following examples contain adjective phrases with a premodifier (58) and with a postmodifier (59); they also illustrate that a premodifier and a postmodifier may occur in combination (60) and that the function of premodifier as well as postmodifier may be realized more than once (61 and 62, respectively):

(58) I am reading an *extremely interesting* book
(59) Peter felt *doubtful about the outcome of the experiment*
(60) You shouldn't be *so very impatient with him*
(61) Mr Crother was *extremely and unexpectedly ill-tempered*
(62) He found it difficult to be *loyal to the company and to his friends*

As we saw in the preceding section, modifiers are optional in the structure of the noun phrase. In adjective phrases they have the same status; they are non-essential elements in the structure of the phrase. There are, however, two exceptions to the rule that modifiers are optional in adjective phrases. The first concerns a group of adjectives which never allow either pre- or postmodification and which, consequently, always constitute one-word adjective phrases. Another characteristic of this group of adjectives is that they can only realize phrase-internal functions. Some of them are:

former:	the former president	mere:	a mere girl
inner:	the inner circle	outer:	outer space
latter:	his latter years	principal:	the principal characters
live:	a live wire	sheer:	sheer luck
main:	the main issue	upper:	the upper storeys

The second group is constituted by a number of adjectives that cannot occur without a modifier; they all require postmodification. Some examples are:

apt (to go wrong)	loath (to do it)
averse (to hard work)	subject (to delays)
fond (of chocolate)	tantamount (to a command)

Like most other phrases, the adjective phrase can realize functions within the structure of other phrases as well as functions on sentence or clause level. The most usual phrase-internal function of the adjective phrase is that of modifier in a noun phrase. Adjective phrases of little complexity usually occur as premodifiers:

(63) a *circular* argument
(64) a *highly volatile* solution
(65) your *extremely sensible* decision
(66) his *very young* wife

As the examples show, adjective phrases used in premodification are usually either one-word phrases or consist of an adjectival head preceded by a one-word intensifier. More complex adjective phrases, especially those with (longer) postmodifiers, are more usually found in postmodification to a noun phrase head:

(67) a possibility *open to everybody*
(68) an opinion *different from yours*
(69) an attitude *firmer than we expected*
(70) people *rich enough to pay that amount of money*

Some adjectives always follow the head of a noun phrase. Postmodification is also regular if the head of the noun phrase is a pronoun. Examples of such adjective phrases in postmodification are given in subsection 6.1.3.

As constituents of clauses or sentences, adjective phrases can only realize the functions subject attribute and object attribute.

Examples:
(71)	The new edition will be *available* in August	: subject attribute
(72)	He is becoming *a bit too big for his boots*	: subject attribute
(73)	It was *quite unnecessary* for you to do that	: subject attribute
(74)	In those days it was thought *indecent* to kiss a girl in public	: subject attribute
(75)	They found the little scene *highly amusing*	: object attribute
(76)	We'd like the sheets *a little cleaner*	: object attribute
(77)	His obstinacy is making the job *unnecessarily difficult*	: object attribute
(78)	It made him *very sad* to see his son in uniform	: object attribute

It should be noted that not all adjectives can function both as immediate constituents of phrases and as constituents of clauses or sentences. Some adjectives can only fill phrase-internal functions, while others can only realize a subject attribute or object attribute function. These two groups of adjectives are discussed and illustrated, as attributive and predicative adjectives respectively, in subsection 2.2.2.

3.4 The adverb phrase

In the internal structure of the adverb phrase the same two functions are distinguished as in the adjective phrase, namely those of head and modifier. A constituent which precedes the head is a premodifier, one that follows the head a postmodifier. The following examples illustrate adverb phrases containing a premodifier (79) and a postmodifier (80); example (81) shows that more than one premodifier is possible, while (82) illustrates an adverb phrase with two postmodifiers.

(79) Tim's sister behaved *hardly less foolishly*
(80) You were driving *faster than 100 m.p.h.*
(81) He turns up *exceedingly and suspiciously often*
(82) We should leave *early enough to catch the 8.15*

The above sentences contain no examples of adverb phrases in which the head is both premodified and postmodified. It is true that there are adverb phrases with constituents before as well as after the head (83 and 84), but in such cases there is always semantic interdependence between the two constituents, so that they had better be looked upon as instances of discontinuous modification.

(83) Such offenders are treated *less tolerantly than in the past*
(84) The problem was discussed *too broadly to provide any real insight*

More examples of discontinuous modification in adverb phrases are given in subsection 6.3.3.

There are a great number of adverbs which occur as one-word adverb phrases only, resisting both pre- and postmodification. These adverbs can be roughly classified into the following groups:

(a) *Adverbs of place*, eg: abroad, ashore, hereabouts, home, in, indoors, out, outdoors, underfoot, underground, underwater.

(b) *Adverbs of time*, eg: afterwards, already, beforehand, eventually, ever, finally, formerly, forthwith, henceforth (-forward), hitherto, lately, latterly, meanwhile, mostly (= as a rule), now, nowadays, originally, presently, still, then, today, tomorrow, tonight, ultimately, yesterday.

(c) *Interrogative adverbs*: how, whither, when, whence, where, why. These adverbs are occasionally modified by intensifying postmodifiers such as *on earth* and by the adverb *ever*.

(d) *Intensifying adverbs and adverbs of degree*, eg: almost, altogether, enough, even, extremely, fairly (= moderately), greatly, hardly, increasingly, most, mostly (= chiefly), only, practically, quite, rather, really, scarcely, somewhat, too, utterly, very, wholly.

(e) *Conjuncts* (see below), eg: accordingly, again, also, alternatively, besides, consequently, conversely, equally, firstly (secondly, etc), furthermore, however, likewise, moreover, namely, nevertheless, next, otherwise, similarly, therefore, yet.

(f) *Other adverbs*, eg: askance, clockwise (edge-, length-), just (= simply), needs, part-time, perhaps, piecemeal, pointblank, reciprocally, somehow, thus, twofold (threefold, etc).

The phrase-internal role played by adverb phrases is, in general, limited to the function of premodifier in the adjective phrase (85–88) and that of premodifier in other adverb phrases (89–92):

(85) *highly* interesting
(86) *exceedingly* dangerous
(87) *quite exceptionally* clever
(88) *almost distressingly* beautiful
(89) *quite* often
(90) *rather* misleadingly
(91) *much too* rapidly
(92) *not quite so* abundantly

Apart from these typical functions some (one-word) adverb phrases can also realize a number of less usual phrase-internal functions:

(a) Premodifier in a noun phrase:
     (93) the *then* president
     (94) an *away* game

(b) Postmodifier in a noun phrase:
     (95) the party *tomorrow*
     (96) the way *ahead*
     (97) the snow *underfoot*
     (98) living conditions *abroad*

(c) The adverb *ever* can function as postmodifier of interrogative *WH*-words (99–100) and as postmodifier in a noun phrase whose head is premodified by a superlative (101–102):
     (99) Who *ever* can have done that?
     (100) What *ever* do you mean?
     (101) the greatest politician *ever*
     (102) the biggest fool *ever*

(d) The adverb *enough* can function as postmodifier in noun phrases (103), adjective phrases (104) and adverb phrases (105):
     (103) We've got milk *enough*
     (104) We are simply not rich *enough*
     (105) He speaks fluently *enough*

(e) Finally, an adverb may be used to premodify a preposition:
     (106) We are *dead* against the proposal
     (107) John is standing *right* behind you
     (108) The attempt was a failure *partly* because of the rain
     (109) The castle must be *just* beyond that hill

As constituents of sentences and clauses, adverb phrases nearly always realize the function adverbial. Three types of adverbial functions can be distinguished: conjuncts, disjuncts and adjuncts. **Conjuncts** function as the connecting link between the sentence in which they occur and the preceding context. **Disjuncts** usually function as 'comment' words, that is, they provide the speaker's comment on the content or form of the utterance. All other adverbs that are constituents of a clause or sentence function as **adjuncts**. Examples:

Conjunct:
(110) John always drives very carefully. *Nevertheless* he had an accident last night
(111) One of my students had promised to meet me at the station. *However*, he was not there
(112) This is a book I would very much like to have. It is very expensive, *though*

Disjunct:
(113) *Frankly*, I don't like him at all
(114) *Seriously*, do you really want to spend your holidays in Spain?
(115) *Briefly*, that is all I have to say on the matter

Adjunct:
(116) Sheila dances *beautifully*
(117) Dr Smith will give that lecture *tomorrow*
(118) The police could not find the missing child *anywhere*

A few adverbs can also, non-typically, occur in the function of subject attribute:

(119) Her husband is *abroad*
(120) The party is *tomorrow*
(121) That should be *enough*
(122) Is John *in*?
(123) They are *together*
(124) He has been *away* for a long time

Only a limited number of adverbs can fill both sentential and phrase-internal functions. Thus most of the intensifying adverbs mentioned above in the list of adverbs resisting modification can only function as premodifier in adjective and adverb phrases; on the other hand, most of the adverbs mentioned under the other categories in that list can normally only function on sentence or clause level. Finally there are some adverbs that can function on phrase as well as on sentence level. Usually, however, there is a clear differentiation of meaning between the two functions. Compare, for example:

(125) a. *Surprisingly*, he turned out to be an honest man
      b. He turned out to be a *surprisingly* honest man
(126) a. *Quite incredibly*, he possesses a large fortune
      b. He possesses a *quite incredibly* large fortune
(127) a. *Oddly*, he remained calm throughout the interrogation
      b. He remained *oddly* calm throughout the interrogation

3.5 The verb phrase

As we saw in section 3.1, a phrase derives its name from the word class to which its head belongs. But whereas it is usually only the head that gives its name to a phrase, in verb phrases all the immediate constituents are, without exception, verbs.

Every verb phrase has a dominant member, which is invariably a lexical verb; the lexical verb is always the last constituent of the phrase. Other, subordinated, constituents precede the lexical verb, and invariably belong to the class of auxiliary, or 'helping', verbs (either modal or primary). There is thus a one-to-one correspondence between function and category within the internal structure of the verb phrase. For this reason no separate function labels are needed for the dominant and the subordinated members of a verb phrase—their function is already indicated by the category labels of the constituent verbs.

The same one-to-one correspondence that is found between function and category in the internal structure of the verb phrase can be observed when we consider the verb phrase as a constituent of the clause or sentence; the verb phrase can realize only one function on sentence level, viz that of predicator (cf subsection 8.3.1).

The verb phrase exhibits a number of features that are not found in any of the other phrase types, viz **aspect**, **voice**, **tense** and **mood**. Of these, aspect and voice can occur in finite as well as non-finite verb phrases; tense and mood are typical features of finite verb phrases only. Another feature of the finite verb phrase is that it often exhibits **concord**, that is agreement in person and/or number between the verb phrase and the subject. We shall first briefly discuss aspect and voice and after that deal with tense, mood and concord in relation to the distinction between finite and non-finite verb phrases. We conclude this section with a table comparing the finite and non-finite verb phrase paradigms.

Aspect

Verb phrases can be marked for two aspects: the **perfective aspect** and the **progressive aspect**. The marker of the perfective aspect is the primary auxiliary *have*, in combination with the *-ed* participle morpheme of the following verb. The semantic function of the perfective aspect is, briefly, to refer to the past time sphere in non-finite verb phrases (128) and to indicate the relevance of a state or event at the moment of speaking in finite verb phrases (129–130). In combination with a past tense it may carry other meanings as well, such as non-factuality in the past (131) or priority in time of one past event to another past event (132). Perfective *have* may co-occur with a modal auxiliary (133) and with the primary auxiliary *be* (134). In the sequence of verb phrase constituents it comes after a modal auxiliary and precedes progressive *be*. Examples:

(128) It is better *to have made* a mistake than not *to have tried* at all
(129) He *has been* with the firm for ten years
(130) How it *has rained*!

(131) If you *had listened* to me, this wouldn't have happened
(132) When we got there, everyone else *had left*
(133) You *might have* come a little earlier
(134) We *have been being* insulted by that man for the past thirty minutes

The marker of the progressive aspect is the primary auxiliary *be*, in combination with the *-ing* participle morpheme of the following verb. From a semantic point of view, we may say that the principal function of the progressive aspect is to express limited duration and hence to emphasize the temporary character of the activity denoted by the lexical verb (135). With some lexical verbs, however, the progressive aspect may also refer to an event in the near future (136). Like *have*, progressive *be* may co-occur with a modal auxiliary (137) and with the other primary auxiliaries except *do* (138–139). In the sequence of verb phrase constituents it follows *have* and precedes passive *be* (134). Examples:

(135) I *am staying* with a friend for the time being
(136) We *are flying* to London tomorrow morning
(137) She *may be* bathing the baby at the moment
(138) The prisoner *must have been* lying
(139) The patient *is being* examined

Voice

The term 'voice' refers to the alternation in the form of verb phrases in pairs of sentences like:

(140) a. A gang of young boys *stole* the money
      b. The money *was stolen* by a gang of young boys

The verb phrase in (140b) is marked for the **passive voice** by the primary auxiliary *be* in combination with the *-ed* participle morpheme of the lexical verb; the unmarked verb phrase in (140a) is said to be in the **active voice**. The semantic function of the passive voice is not, as in the case of progressive and perfective aspect, to add an element of meaning, but rather to change the semantic role of the subject constituent. In a sentence with a passive verb phrase the subject constituent takes on the semantic role that is otherwise performed by the object constituent in a corresponding sentence with an active verb phrase (often that of 'victim'). Compare:

(141) a. Macbeth murdered *the king*
      b. *The king* was murdered by Macbeth

As example (141b) shows, the semantic function of the subject constituent in a sentence with an active verb phrase (often that of 'agent'), is shifted to an adverbial introduced by the preposition *by*, when the verb phrase is marked for the passive voice. Very often, however, this semantic role is dropped altogether:

(142) The murderer was arrested last night
(143) That point will be discussed at the next meeting

Since the effect of the passive voice is a change in the semantic value of other constituents of the sentence than the verb phrase, the terms active and passive are not only applied to verb phrases, but also to the sentences in which they occur.

A verb phrase can only be marked for the passive if it contains a transitive complement verb, ie a verb that in its active form requires an object constituent. This means that the following types of lexical verbs can occur in the passive voice: monotransitive verbs (144), ditransitive verbs (145–146), complex transitive verbs (147) and transitive PC verbs (148). Examples:

(144) The soldier was hit by shrapnel
(145) This book was given me by my sister
(146) I was given this book by my sister
(147) Jim has been appointed head of the department
(148) The play should not be compared with *Hamlet*

As can be seen from examples (145–146), the subject constituent in a sentence containing a ditransitive verb may either correspond to the direct object or to the indirect object constituent of an analogous active sentence. Compare:

(149) *This book* was given me by my sister—My sister gave me *this book*
(150) *I* was given this book by my sister—My sister gave *me* this book

Passive *be* may co-occur with a modal auxiliary and with the other primary auxiliaries except *do*. In the sequence of the verb phrase it immediately precedes the lexical verb.

Finite and non-finite verb phrases

Finite verb phrases contain a finite verbal form, whereas **non-finite** ones do not. Finite verbal forms are those which are morphologically marked for the category of tense and which may, in addition, be marked for the categories of mood and concord. The form *(he) writes*, for example, is marked for all three categories. It is marked for tense because it contrasts with *(he) wrote*, for mood because it contrasts with *(he) write*, and for concord because it contrasts with *(I/you/we/they) write*. A form like *may*, on the other hand, is marked for tense only since it merely shows a morphological contrast with *might*.

Tense

Tense is an obligatory category in the finite verb phrase. We distinguish two tenses in English: the **present tense** and the **past tense**. Tense is always marked on the first verbal form. Compare:

writes:	wrote
may write:	might write
has been writing:	had been writing

Mood

English has three moods: the **indicative mood**, the **subjunctive mood** and the **imperative mood**. The subjunctive and the imperative are morphologically identical with the base:

Subjunctive: (151) God *save* the Queen!
              (152) *Come* what may, we shall not give in
              (153) We insist that she *leave* tomorrow
              (154) The police demand that they *be* informed at once

Imperative: (155) *Get* on with your work
              (156) *Take* care of yourself
              (157) *Mind* the step
              (158) *Repeat* that please, John

The indicative mood is not morphologically distinct from the base with the exception of the third person singular present tense of lexical verbs, which is marked by a sibilant-suffix:

Table 3.2

	Indicative	Subjunctive
I, you, we, they	write	write
he/she/it	writes	write

The difference between the indicative and the subjunctive is best illustrated by means of the verb *be*, which, of all English verbs, has the largest number of different forms:

Table 3.3

		Present tense		Past tense	
		Indicative	Subjunctive	Indicative	Subjunctive
I	am		be	was	were
you	are		be	were	were
he	is		be	was	were
we	are		be	were	were
you	are		be	were	were
they	are		be	were	were

Concord

Concord in the finite verb phrase is agreement in person and/or number between the subject of the sentence and the finite verb. We find concord of number in the following sentences, where a singular subject requires a singular verb and a plural subject requires a plural verb:

(159) a. The boy loves to go to school
       b. The boys love to go to school

Concord of person and number occurs in:

(160) I am a socialist
(161) He is a communist
(162) He lives in London

In Table 3.4 the finite and non-finite verb phrase paradigms are compared:

Table 3.4

Finite verb phrase	Non-finite verb phrase	
	Infinitive	-ing Participle
writes	to write	writing
does write	....	....
is written	to be written	being written
is writing	to be writing	....
has written	to have written	having written
may write	....	....
may have written	....	....
has been writing	to have been writing	having been writing
is being written	to be being written	....
may be writing	....	....
may be written	....	....
has been written	to have been written	having been written
may have been writing	....	....
may have been written	....	....
has been being written	to have been being written (rare)	having been being written (rare)
may be being written	....	....
may have been being written (rare)	....	....

Most of the gaps in the non-finite verb phrase paradigm are due to the fact that modal auxiliaries lack non-finite forms. Note also that there are no non-finite verb phrases containing periphrastic or emphatic *do*. *Do* in these functions is always finite, the only forms available being *do*, *does* and *did*. It is difficult to explain two further gaps in the paradigm: *being writing* and *being being written*, corresponding to *to be writing* and *to be being written*, respectively. As the following examples illustrate, a phrase like *being writing* is replaced by *writing*, while, instead of *being being written* we find *being written*:

(163) a.   While he was writing the letter, he listened to the radio
      b.   *While *being writing* the letter, he listened to the radio
      c.   While *writing* the letter, he listened to the radio

(164) a.   While *it was being written*, the letter became more and more sarcastic
      b.   *While *being being written*, the letter became more and more sarcastic
      c.   While *being written*, the letter became more and more sarcastic

3.6 The prepositional phrase

The structure of the prepositional phrase is determined by its two functions: **prepositional** and **prepositional complement**. The constituent realizing the former governs the one realizing the latter. Both functions are obligatory and they usually occur immediately after each other:

(165) *At five o'clock* we had covered half the distance
(166) They are selling the old types *at exceedingly low prices*
(167) The oak *behind the pond* seems to be dying

The immediate constituents of prepositional phrases that function on clause or sentence level may, under certain conditions, be found in different places in the clause or sentence, the prepositional complement occurring in initial position and the prepositional after the predicate or in final position. This detachment of the two immediate constituents of a prepositional phrase may take place in the following cases:

1. In *WH*-sentences and in *WH*-clauses functioning as constituents of sentences. When the sentence is simple, it is either interrogative (168–169) or exclamatory (170–171). *WH*-clauses with postposed prepositions can fulfil most of the major sentence functions; they may be finite (172–174) as well as non-finite (175–176):

   (168) Who are you going to Spain with?
   (169) Which minister will the bridge be opened by?
   (170) What a silly conclusion they have arrived at!
   (171) What a drag you're letting yourself in for!

   (172) *What they argued about* is not very clear
   (173) Don't you know yet *what you are going to write about*?
   (174) I wonder *what he is going to talk about*
   (175) I really don't know *who to listen to*
   (176) Her problem is *who to sleep with*

2. In finite and non-finite clauses functioning as postmodifier in noun phrases (177–179) and in non-finite postmodifying clauses in adjective phrases (180–181). In such clauses the prepositional complement is often ellipted. Usually ellipsis is optional; this is indicated in the following examples by putting the prepositional complement in parentheses. In (179) and (181) ellipsis is obligatory.

   (177) *My father, who everyone thought most highly of*, died in 1967
   (178) *The kind of girl (that) you are talking about* does not marry at eighteen
   (179) *The man to do business with* is Donald McLeod
   (180) I was *dubious who to ask for*
   (181) The girl turned out to be *worth waiting for*

3. Detachment of the two immediate constituents of a prepositional phrase may take place in a finite (182) or non-finite (183) clause functioning as prepositional complement:

(182) So far, we have only been concerned *with what plan we should give preference to*

(183) The committee have been very hesitant *about who to give the job to*

Typical phrase-internal functions of the prepositional phrase are found in the noun phrase (184-185) and in the adjective phrase (186-187); in both it functions as a postmodifier:

(184) the top *of the table*

(185) a road *through the jungle*

(186) satisfied *with everything*

(187) astonished *at what he had achieved*

Less typically a prepositional phrase may occur as a postmodifier in an adverb phrase (188-189) and as prepositional complement in another prepositional phrase, which is usually introduced by *from* (190-192):

(188) out *in the cold*

(189) away *from home*

(190) from *behind the curtain*

(191) from *within the room*

(192) since *before the war*

As an immediate constituent of the sentence or clause, the prepositional phrase usually functions as adverbial, either as adjunct (193), as conjunct (194) or as disjunct (195):

(193) John will be back *by the end of the month*

(194) I know £10 is not much. *On the other hand*, it should be enough to buy her a present

(195) *In all frankness*, I don't think he is the right man for the job

Less usually, a prepositional phrase may occur as subject (196), as subject attribute (197), as object attribute (198) or as predicator complement (199):

(196) *After the fifteenth of February* would suit me better

(197) Harry was *in high spirits*

(198) She tied the ribbon *into a bow*

(199) The scene reminded me *of my days in the army*

4. The sentence

4.1 Introductory

The morpheme is regarded as the minimal unit of grammatical description since it cannot be segmented any further at the grammatical level of analysis. The sentence is placed at the other extreme of the rank scale and regarded as the largest unit of grammatical description since it does not function in the structure of a unit higher than itself. To treat the sentence as the highest unit implies that we do not take into account larger stretches of language such as paragraphs and texts. This is the domain of text grammar or discourse analysis. Sections 4.2, 4.3 and 4.4 mainly deal with sentences as syntactic structures. Sections 4.5 and 4.6 are concerned with the ways in which sentences function in communication and the ways in which speakers manipulate the structure of sentences in order to organize their messages.

Sentences can be described by specifying:

1. the **functions** that their constituents have in sentence structure
2. the **categories** to which their constituents belong

For example, the four constituents in

(1) All students should have read this article by Monday

can be described as follows:

		function	*category*
all students	:	subject (Su)	NP
should have read:		predicator (P)	VP
this article	:	direct object (DO)	NP
by Monday	:	adverbial (A)	Prep. P.

As we shall see in Chapter 7, it is necessary to specify both function and category at the same time, as in:

(1) a. All students – should have read – this article – by Monday
        [Su: NP]   [P: VP]   [DO: NP]   [A: Prep. P.]

Apart from the functions subject (Su), predicator (P), direct object (DO) and adverbial (A), we also distinguish the functions indirect object (IO), benefactive object (BO), subject attribute (SA), object attribute (OA) and predicator complement (PC). Sentence functions are dealt with in Chapter 7. Categories (such as NP and VP) are dealt with in Chapters 3 and 6.

Additional examples:

(2) Professor Smith – has offered – my brother – a job
        [Su: NP]   [P: VP]   [IO: NP]   [DO: NP]

(3) Joyce's baby – has fallen – ill
    [Su: NP]   [P: VP]   [SA: Adj. P.]

(4) That remark – made – me – sick
    [Su: NP]   [P: VP]   [DO: NP] [OA: Adj. P.]

Rankshift

So far we have assumed that the sentence, being the largest unit of grammatical description, does not function in the structure of a unit higher than itself. However, two further possibilities should be mentioned. First, a sentence can function in the structure of another sentence, that is in the structure of a unit of the same rank. Secondly, a sentence can function in the structure of a phrase, that is in the structure of a unit lower than itself (cf also subsection 0.2.7).

Examples:

Sentence in structure of sentence: (5) I believe *that he is honest*
                                    (6) *What Jack says* is true

Sentence in structure of phrase   : (7) Do you know the man *who came to dinner*?
                                    (8) I am very glad *that you are here*
                                    (9) She was afraid of *what might happen next*

Sentences that are embedded in the structure of other sentences or in the structure of phrases are called **clauses**. Clauses can have other clauses embedded in them (see subsection 4.3.1.1).

4.2 The simple sentence

A **simple sentence** can be defined as a sentence in which none of the functions is realized by a clause. In other words, a simple sentence does not contain an embedded (or subordinate) sentence as realization of one of its functions. A simple sentence is always an independent sentence, that is a sentence capable of occurring on its own. If we compare (10a) with (10b–h), it is obvious that (10a) can be used independently but that (10b–h) cannot:

(10) a. John is a bachelor

(10) b. that John is a bachelor
     c. why John is a bachelor
     d. whether John is a bachelor
     e. though John is a bachelor
     f. because John is a bachelor
     g. (for) John to be a bachelor
     h. John being a bachelor

The following are additional examples of simple sentences:

(11) The children have been quarrelling all day
(12) Peter has grown a moustache
(13) The two men were arrested in a pub last night
(14) John's father is a civil servant
(15) We came to the conclusion that a conflict was inevitable
(16) The conclusion that we came to was inevitable
(17) Jack was very glad that he had passed his exam
(18) She was afraid of leaving the children alone at night
(19) An hour later we made another attempt to cross the river

In spite of the fact that (15-19) contain clauses, they should be regarded as simple. The reason is that the finite *that*-clauses in (15), (16) and (17) and the non-finite clauses in (18) and (19) do not function as constituents of the sentence, but are embedded in a noun phrase (15, 16 and 19), an adjective phrase (17) and a prepositional phrase (18). Additional examples of simple sentences containing clauses are the following:

Clause in structure of noun phrase:
    finite   : (20) Is this the book *that Jane lent you*?
    non-finite: (21) There is no reason *to be upset*

Clause in structure of adjective phrase:
    finite   : (22) She was very pleased *that we had come*
    non-finite: (23) I am inclined *to believe that story*

Clause in structure of adverb phrase:
    finite   : (24) He drove so fast *that the car skidded*
    non-finite: (25) Jim behaved so strangely *as to frighten everybody*

Clause in structure of prepositional phrase:
    finite   : (26) Are you surprised at *what he said*?
    non-finite: (27) He is very good at *playing poker*

4.3 Combining and condensing sentences

A comparison of the (a) and (b) examples below shows that sentences can be combined by means of two syntactic devices in English syntax: **subordination** and **coordination**:

(28) a. I remember. I saw the jewels
     b. I remember seeing the jewels
(29) a. Jack is a bachelor. His sister is married
     b. Jack is a bachelor but his sister is married

Examples (30b) and (31b) illustrate that English also has two devices (**substitution** and **ellipsis**) that enable speakers to condense sentences in order to avoid repetition:

(30) a. Peter said that Peter wanted to go home
     b. Peter said that he wanted to go home

(31) a. Frank reads English at Cambridge and Anne reads English at Durham
  b. Frank reads English at Cambridge and Anne at Durham

4.3.1 *Subordination and coordination*

Subordination (or embedding) and coordination are two syntactic means that speakers use in order to combine propositions that would otherwise have to be stated in strings of independent sentences. Subordination involves the use of a sentence as an element in the structure of another sentence. Figures 4.1 and 4.2 represent sentences in which another sentence (*that he was not killed*) has been embedded and functions as subject and direct object respectively:

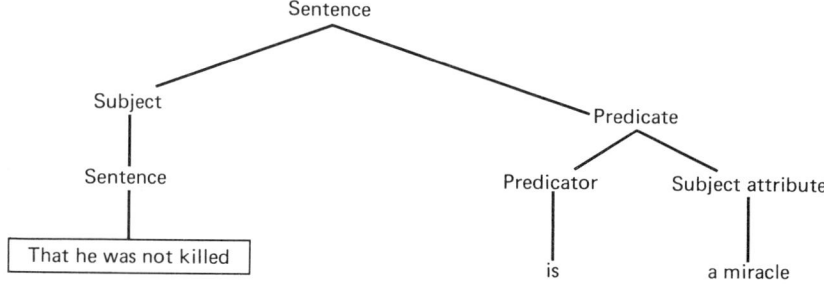

Figure 4.1

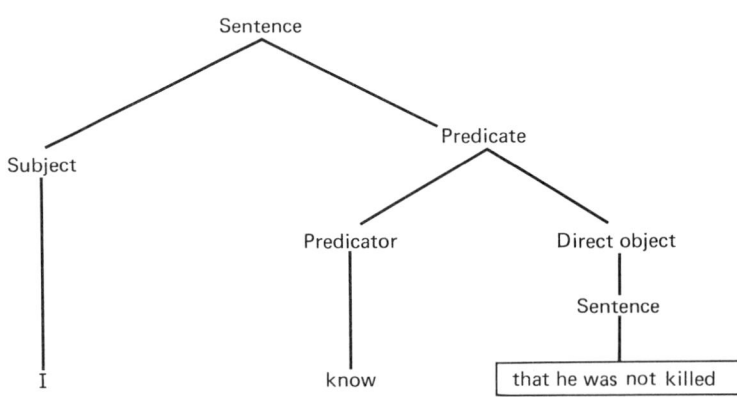

Figure 4.2

Coordination involves the linking of two or more sentences, as illustrated in Figures 4.3–4.5:

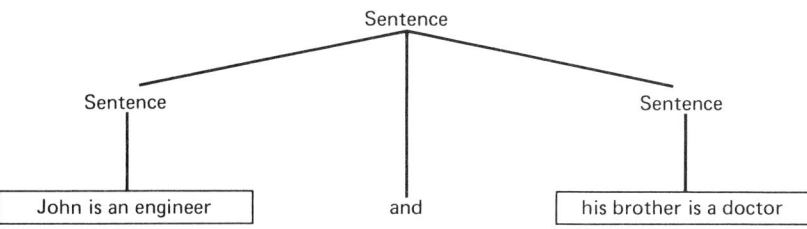

Figure 4.3

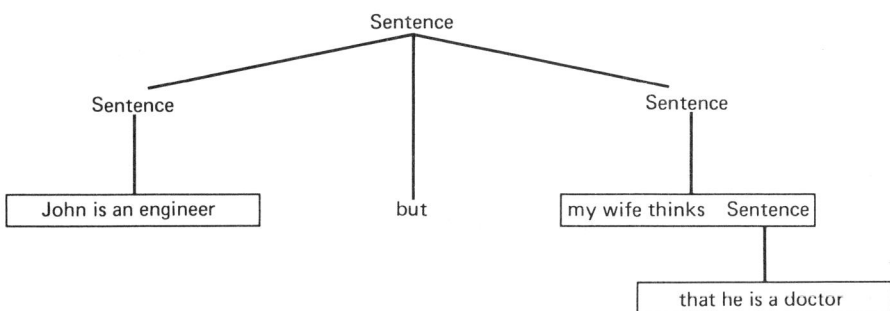

Figure 4.4

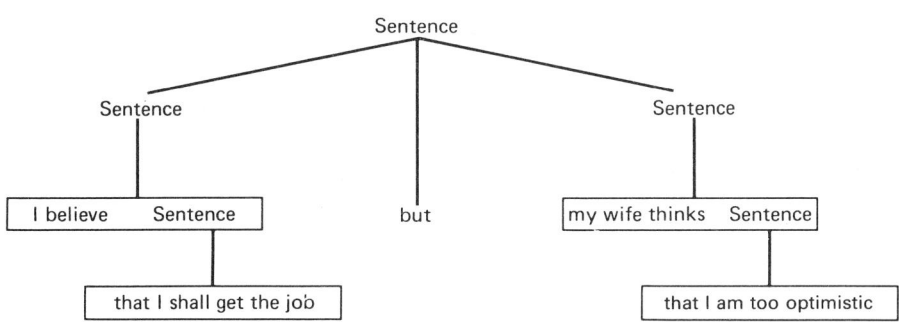

Figure 4.5

Sentences involving subordination (with the exception of the type exemplified by (15–27) above) are called **complex**. Those involving coordination are called **compound**.

4.3.1.1 The complex sentence

Sentences in which one or more sentence functions are realized by a clause (finite or non-finite) are complex. A sentence or clause that contains one or more clauses is called **superordinate**. Each of the examples below contains only one embedded clause:

(32) *That the baby is ill* is obvious
(33) *To do that* would be foolish
(34) I believe *that she is English*
(35) Do you remember *him saying that*?
(36) The problem is *that we have no money*
(37) His first duty is *to look after you*
(38) *If you do that*, you will be fired
(39) *Being ill*, I cannot come
(40) *As he said this*, the door opened

The following complex sentences contain more than one clause:

(41) *That Jim is not here* probably means *that he has overslept*
(42) *What you say* implies *that you do not approve*
(43) *Being very intelligent*, he quickly understood *what we were up to*
(44) *What matters* is *that he has confidence in us*
(45) *As he was watching her*, he suddenly realized *how pretty she was*

As sentences (46–49) show, clauses can, in turn, contain more deeply embedded clauses:

(46) I wonder *if you would care to tell me why you think that George deserves being promoted*
(47) I do not mind *telling you that I am bored as soon as I come home*
(48) She was angry *because she resented him going away*
(49) You must admit *that you knew that I had told my father that I am pregnant*

Note that sentences (46–49) contain more than one superordinate clause. In (49), for example, the whole sentence (*a*) is superordinate to clause *b*. Clause *b*, in turn, is superordinate to clause *c*, which is superordinate to clause *d* (see Figure 4.6).

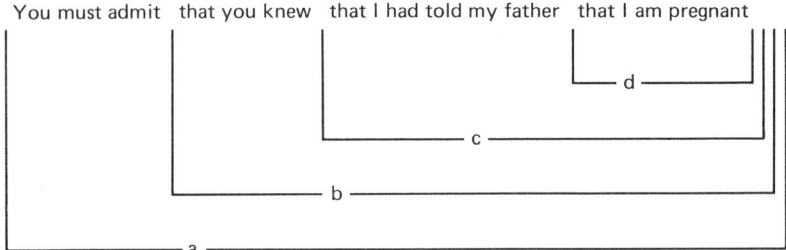

Figure 4.6

Clauses can be classified in two ways. From a structural point of view we can distinguish three types:

1. finite clauses
2. non-finite clauses
3. verbless clauses

Finite clauses contain a finite verb phrase, that is a verb phrase capable of showing tense, mood, aspect and voice. Examples:

(50) *That Henry avoids you* is understandable
(51) We discovered *who sent the letter*
(52) The question was *why Mabel was not interested*

Non-finite clauses contain a non-finite verb phrase (an infinitive, an *-ing* participle or an *-ed* participle), which cannot show tense or mood. Examples:

(53) *To say that in public* is dangerous
(54) I don't remember *saying that*
(55) *The job finished*, we went to the pub

Verbless clauses do not contain a verbal form. They often consist of a noun phrase or adjective phrase only. Frequently they lack a subject and they may be looked upon as clauses in which a form of the verb *be* has been omitted. Examples:

(56) *A staunch liberal*, George did not believe in state ownership
(57) *Although a staunch liberal*, George believed in state ownership
(58) *Always a staunch liberal*, George did not believe in state ownership

In (56) there would seem to be no reason at first sight to call *A staunch liberal* a clause rather than a phrase. Comparison with (57) and (58), however, shows that the possibility of adding items like *although* (subordinator) or *always* (adverb phrase) enables us to label *A staunch liberal* in (56) as a clause. Sentences (56–58) can therefore be paraphrased as follows:

(56) a. George was a staunch liberal and he did not believe in state ownership
(57) a. Although George was a staunch liberal, he believed in state ownership
(58) a. George had always been a staunch liberal and he did not believe in state ownership

Additional examples of verbless clauses are:

(59) *Unable to make up his mind*, he looked at us in silence
(60) *Their hands deep in their pockets*, the spectators were watching the game

The second way of classifying clauses is in terms of the functions they can play in the structure of the sentence. We can distinguish the following types:

1. subject clauses
2. direct object clauses
3. indirect object clauses
4. benefactive object clauses
5. subject attribute clauses
6. object attribute clauses
7. predicator complement clauses
8. adverbial clauses

With the exception of the indirect object and the benefactive object sentence functions can be realized by both finite and non-finite clauses. The function adverbial can, in addition, be realized by a verbless clause. Examples (for additional examples see Chapter 8):

Subject clause:
    finite   : (61) *That this book is out of print* surprises me
    non-finite: (62) *Having breakfast in bed* is rather nice

Direct object clause:
    finite   : (63) My neighbour believes *that his wife is unfaithful*
    non-finite: (64) I don't know *what to do*

Indirect object clause:
    finite   : (65) She gave *whoever came in* an angry look

Benefactive object clause:
    finite   : (66) The man bought *whoever came in* a beer

Subject attribute clause:
    finite   : (67) My feeling is *that this cannot be right*
    non-finite: (68) Our first task will be *to expand our foreign trade*

Object attribute clause:
    finite   : (69) My uncle made that firm *what it is today*
    non-finite: (70) I call that *killing two birds with one stone*

Predicator complement clause:
    finite   : (71) Would you mind *if I came at six*?
    non-finite: (72) I fail *to see your point*

Adverbial clause:
    finite   : (73) *If he believes that*, he must be mad
    non-finite: (74) *To speak frankly*, I don't like her
    verbless : (75) *A very disappointed man*, he left early

As the examples above show, there are three ways to indicate that a clause is embedded in a sentence:

1. the clause contains a non-finite verb phrase,
2. the clause is introduced by subordinators like *if*, *as*, *though*, etc,
3. the clause is introduced by the word *that* or by WH-words like *who*, *why*, *whether*, etc.

4.3.1.2 The compound sentence

A compound sentence is one in which two or more sentences (called conjoins) have been coordinated. Each of the conjoins is independent, since there is no question of embedding. Coordination may be **asyndetic**, in which case it is not marked overtly. Examples:

(76) He was a moody man, his temper was never equable
(77) Brooks was a brilliant chemist, he was ten years ahead of his time

Coordination is usually **syndetic** (at least if two sentences are involved), being indicated by means of one of the coordinators *and*, *or*, *for* and *but*. As Table 4.1 shows, a compound sentence may consist of:

1. two (or more) simple sentences (cf Figure 4.3),
2. one (or more) simple sentences + one (or more) complex sentences (cf Figure 4.4),
3. two (or more) complex sentences (cf Figure 4.5).

Table 4.1

	simple sentence + simple sentence (+ simple sentence . . .)	Exs. 78–84
The compound sentence	any combination of simple and complex sentences	Exs. 85–91
	complex sentence + complex sentence (+ complex sentence . . .)	Exs. 92–97

Examples:

(78) Oil is now more expensive and that will affect our economy
(79) I have bought a new shirt, but it does not fit me
(80) Can you come to dinner on Saturday or are you busy?
(81) Peter must be ill, for he did not turn up
(82) Frank is a psychologist, David is a teacher, and Robert is reading English at Cambridge
(83) We had got up at six, the taxi was in time, but still we missed our train
(84) You could go to France, we could go to Spain, or we could all go to Greece

(85) I know that he feels depressed but has he taken his pills?
(86) Saskia believes that I am in love with her and she is right
(87) John is a very sensible chap but he says that he cannot agree to our plans
(88) Longmans will publish that book in the spring or do you think that is too late?
(89) The police believe that the car was stolen for they cannot find it
(90) She likes being teased, but she does not show it
(91) I hear that he is sympathetic to the régime, but that does not worry me

(92) He must have believed what I said about the club and that is why he joined
(93) I wish he would tell me the truth but I know he is a coward
(94) The neighbours complained that the music was too loud and so they decided to ring the police
(95) I remember dancing with a lot of girls, but I don't know if Anne was there
(96) Joan admits that she had a lot of money in the bank, but she claims that she has lost everything
(97) We would prefer him not to go or do you think it is necessary?

4.3.2 *Substitution and ellipsis*

In order to avoid repetition (both across sentences and within sentences) two grammatical devices are used: substitution and ellipsis. Substitution may be defined as the replacement of one or more items by a substitute or **pro-form**. It is illustrated by the following pairs of examples:

(98) a. **Melissa* said that *Melissa* wanted to study at Cambridge
       b. Melissa said that she wanted to study at Cambridge
(99) a. **Charles *came to Paris in the spring* and Peter *came to Paris in the spring*
       b. Charles came to Paris in the spring and so did Peter

Ellipsis enables us to abbreviate sentences by omitting elements that are retrievable from the context. The process is illustrated by the following examples:

(100) a. We had invited Robin *to come to the party* but he did not want *to come to the party*
       b. We had invited Robin to come to the party but he did not want to
(101) a. Paul *bought* a dictionary and Harry *bought* an anthology
       b. Paul bought a dictionary and Harry an anthology

4.3.2.1 Substitution

In English pro-forms are used to replace:

1. a noun phrase
2. an adjective phrase
3. a verb phrase
4. a clause

Pro-forms to replace a noun phrase

Noun phrases can be replaced by the pro-forms *he*, *she*, *it*, *we*, *you* (plural) and *they*, by possessive and reflexive pronouns, by the words *one* and *ones* (which replace count nouns or noun phrases with count nouns as head) and by *that* and *those*.

Examples:

(102) *The children* saw *that film* but *they* did not like *it*
(103) This is *Fred's* car and here are *his* keys
(104) *Mary* is not *herself* these days
(105) This *sentence* is easier to analyse than the *one* on the previous page
(106) I love red *roses* but she prefers white *ones*
(107) My tutor likes Yeats's *poetry*, but I prefer *that* of Keats
(108) *The canals* of Venice are more beautiful than *those* of Amsterdam

Pro-forms to replace an adjective phrase

Adjective phrases functioning as subject attribute or object attribute can be replaced by the pro-forms *so* and *that*, which are used together with the verb *be*:

(109) The boys promised to be *good* and *so* they were
(110) Simon had been described as *very intelligent* and *that* he certainly was

Pro-forms to replace a verb phrase

Verb phrases (often together with other elements of the sentence) can be replaced by *do, do so, do it, do that, so do* and *so . . . do* (on the difference between *so do* and *so . . . do* see subsection 2.2.9.8). Examples:

(111) Mary *snores* and Gerry *does*, too
(112) Bob promised *to meet us at the airport* and he *did*
(113) John's parents *bought a boat last year* and mine *did so*, too
(114) Nancy *left her husband* but nobody knows why she *did that*
(115) I *smoke 20 cigarettes a day* and *so does* my wife
(116) Your brother *drinks too much. So* he *does*

Pro-forms to replace a clause

The pro-forms *so, not, it, this* and *that* can be used to substitute for clauses as in:

(117) *Are the girls coming to the party?* I hope *so*
(118) Do you think *there is going to be a strike*? I believe *so*
(119) *Has your secretary gone home*? It seems *so*
(120) The papers say that *the President is ill*. If *so*, why does not he resign?
(121) *Is Douglas coming too*? I hope *not*
(122) John told me that *he had failed his exam* but *it* did not come as a surprise to me
(123) *They have spent all their money* and *this* was to be expected
(124) *He is now going to divorce his wife* but *that* is another story

The words *here, there, now, then* and *that* may be regarded as pro-forms replacing adverbial expressions of place and time. Examples:

(125) We were to meet *at the corner of Dean Street and Shaftesbury Avenue* but she was not *there*
(126) The baby was rushed to hospital *on Sunday* but *then* it was too late
(127) They are going *next year* but *that* is not the best time

4.3.2.2 Ellipsis

The difference between substitution and ellipsis is that in the case of ellipsis a structural slot is not filled by a pro-form (as in substitution), but remains empty. A condition is that the ellipted material can be recovered either from the linguistic context, as in

(128) John is not likely to come, but he might (come)

or from the non-linguistic context, as in

(129) (Would you) care for a drink, Jim?

Ellipsis is such a complex phenomenon that a detailed treatment would be beyond the scope of this book. The examples below illustrate cases of ellipsis in sentences in linguistic contexts only.

Ellipsis involving the subject only

(130) Many students love languages but (many students) are not interested in science
(131) He believed that he was right and (he) was not prepared to apologize
(132) The book is important and (the book) can be recommended to everybody interested in language

Ellipsis involving the subject and (part(s) of) the predicator

(133) The children should have been told what to do and (the children should have been told) where to go
(134) We have given Mary flowers and (we have given) John a bottle of whisky
(135) Ronald wrote a book on Henry VIII and (Ronald wrote) another on Elizabeth I
(136) They could go to the British Museum or (they could) visit the National Gallery
(137) The strikers could (have been fired) and (the strikers) should have been fired

Ellipsis involving (part(s) of) the predicator

(138) My parents will be going to Spain and Susan's parents (will be going) to Morocco
(139) The boy should have been punished and the girl (should have been) rewarded
(140) He said he had not been swimming, but he had (been swimming)
(141) Though Jane has tried, Fred has not (tried)
(142) Peter loves Beethoven, Frank (loves) Schubert and Sally (loves) Brahms

Ellipsis involving (part(s) of) the predicator and a complement or adverbial

(143) Peter teaches linguistics at Harvard and Virginia (teaches linguistics) at Yale
(144) My son has been advised to leave the country and he might (leave the country)
(145) He promised that he would write the essay but has he (written the essay)?

(146) Professor Smith was Head of the Department last year and Professor Robins (was Head of the Department) in 1980
(147) We are not going to France, but the children are (going to France)

Ellipsis involving a complement or an adverbial only

(148) Fred imports (used cars) and his father sells used cars
(149) He promises to be (a first-rate scientist) and his brother already is a first-rate scientist
(150) Fred lives (in London) and his girlfriend works in London
(151) I thought he was in his study but he was not (in his study)

4.4 Negation and the formation of questions

Negative and interrogative sentences in English are formed in ways that are best illustrated by starting out from their positive declarative counterparts.

4.4.1 *Negation*

Negative sentences contain the word *not* (or its contracted form *-n't*), which occurs after the first auxiliary. Examples:

(152) John may have written that letter — John may not have written that letter
(153) We are going to Mary's wedding — We are not going to Mary's wedding
(154) The meeting will be cancelled — The meeting will not be cancelled
(155) You should have paid some attention to her — You shouldn't have paid any attention to her
(156) I have finished already — I have not finished yet

Note that *some* and *already* in (155) and (156) are replaced by *any* and *yet* in the corresponding negative sentences. Compare also examples (171) and (174) on questions.

If the positive declarative sentence does not contain an auxiliary, periphrastic *do* must be used. Examples:

(157) They work very hard — They don't work very hard
(158) John got his degree in 1980 — John did not get his degree in 1980
(159) Mary lives in London — Mary does not live in London

Negative imperative sentences require periphrastic *do*. Those containing *let's* have two variants:

(160) Open that window — Don't open that window
(161) Let's go now — Don't let's go now
　　　　　　　　　　　Let's not go now

In negative imperative sentences periphrastic *do* is also used with the verb *be*:

(162) Don't be silly!
(163) Don't be offended!

Negative sentences containing *dare, need* and *used* have two variants. Cf:

(164) He dares to challenge me   – He daren't challenge me
        He does not dare (to) challenge me
(165) You need to be cautious   – You needn't be cautious
        You don't need to be cautious
(166) The family used to be rich   – The family usedn't to be rich
        The family did not use(d) to be rich

Negative sentences containing the lexical verb *have* in the meaning of 'possess' have three variants. See examples (167) and (168). Many speakers look upon the first variant as formal and stilted. The construction with *got* is particularly frequent in colloquial English. In the past tense the variant with *did* is preferred. American English prefers the *do*-construction both in the present and in the past tense. Cf:

(167) I have a car   – I haven't a car
        I don't have a car
        I haven't got a car
(168) She had a good memory   – She hadn't a good memory
        She didn't have a good memory
        She hadn't got a good memory

Other meanings of lexical *have* require periphrastic *do*. Examples:

(169) They have breakfast at 8   – They don't have breakfast at 8
(170) The children had a nice time   – The children didn't have a nice time

4.4.2 *The formation of questions*

We distinguish two main types of questions: **yes/no questions** (including tag-questions) and **WH-questions**.

Yes/no questions are formed by putting the first auxiliary in front of the subject:

(171) The children have been punished already   – Have the children been punished yet?
(172) She should have told us   – Should she have told us?
(173) The Prime Minister is being interviewed on TV   – Is the Prime Minister being interviewed on TV?
(174) Jack would be willing to lend us some money   – Would Jack be willing to lend us any money?

If the corresponding declarative sentence does not contain an auxiliary, periphrastic *do* must be used. Examples:

(175) Professor Grant lives in Canterbury   – Does Professor Grant live in Canterbury?

(176) You believed what I said   – Did you believe what I said?

Yes/no questions containing *dare*, *need* and *used* have two variants. Cf:

(177) She dares to ride a motor-bike   – Dare she ride a motorbike? Does she dare (to) ride a motorbike?

(178) Judges need to be impartial   – Need judges be impartial? Do judges need to be impartial?

(179) His daughters used to be beautiful   – Used his daughters to be beautiful? Did his daughters use(d) to be beautiful?

In yes/no questions the behaviour of the lexical verb *have*, in the meaning of 'possess' as well as in other meanings, is similar to that in negative sentences. Cf:

(180) Mary has 5 children   – Has Mary 5 children? Has Mary got 5 children? Does Mary have 5 children?

(181) She had blue eyes   – Had she blue eyes? Had she got blue eyes? Did she have blue eyes?

(182) They had lamb for dinner   – Did they have lamb for dinner?

Tag-questions consist of a statement, followed by a question. The subject of the tag is always a pronoun which either repeats or replaces the subject of the statement. The first auxiliary of the statement is repeated in the tag, but if the statement contains a lexical verb in the present or past tense, a form of the auxiliary *do* must be used. Positive statements are normally followed by negative tags and vice versa. Examples:

(183) Simon should have known better, shouldn't he?

(184) It might have been dangerous, mightn't it?

(185) He does not like women, does he?

(186) Queen Victoria died in 1901, didn't she?

In *WH*-questions a *WH*-item occurs in initial position. Examples (188–192) show that the subject follows the first auxiliary (or a form of periphrastic *do*), except when the *WH*-item functions as subject (187):

(187) Oscar will be held respon-sible   – Who will be held responsible?

(188) We could borrow John's book   – Whose book could we borrow?

(189) She prefers the red one   – Which one does she prefer?

(190) The plane lands at 6   – When does the plane land?
(191) He had repaired it with a   – How had he repaired it?
      piece of string
(192) She left because she felt   – Why did she leave?
      unwell

4.5 Grammatical form and function in communication

In sections 4.2 and 4.3 we saw that in terms of their structural complexity sentences can be divided into three types: simple sentences, complex sentences and compound sentences. This section deals with two different classifications of sentences. The first is based on their **grammatical form**, the second on their **function in communication**.

4.5.1 *Sentences and their grammatical form*

This classification comprises four types: declarative sentences, interrogative sentences, imperative sentences and exclamatory sentences.

Declarative sentences

Declarative sentences always have a subject, which precedes the verb. Examples:

(193) Paris is the capital of France
(194) Dr Johnson's Dictionary was published in 1755
(195) This passage illustrates his sense of humour
(196) In 1950 my parents emigrated to Australia

Interrogative sentences

Interrogative sentences contain a subject and open with an auxiliary verb or a *WH*-word. Examples:

(197) Does your mother know about this?
(198) Can you play Scarlatti?
(199) Who wrote this letter?
(200) What did he tell you?

Sentences (197) and (198) are examples of so-called yes/no questions, that is questions requiring *yes* or *no* for an answer. Sentences (199) and (200) exemplify *WH*-questions, which require a piece of information for an answer.

A second type of yes/no question is the so-called tag-question, which consists of a statement with a question appended to it, as in:

(201) John should work harder, shouldn't he?
(202) She could not have finished her essay, could she?
(203) Your children admire him, don't they?

Imperative sentences

Imperative sentences contain a verb in the imperative mood. If a subject is present it is usually *you*, but as a rule the subject is lacking. Examples:

(204) Shut that door at once
(205) Find me another pencil
(206) Be there in time, please
(207) You go in first

Exclamatory sentences

In **exclamatory sentences** the subject precedes the verb. They are introduced by phrases opening with the words *how* or *what*. Examples:

(208) How beautiful she is!
(209) How brave you are!
(210) What a crashing bore he is!
(211) What a good teacher Jim would make!

4.5.2 *Sentences and their function in communication*

The four sentence types discussed in subsection 4.5.1 may be said to be primarily associated with one particular function in speech situations. Declarative sentences are chiefly used to make **statements**, interrogative sentences to ask **questions**, imperative sentences to give **commands** and exclamatory sentences to make **exclamations** (see Table 4.2).

Table 4.2

Grammatical form	Function in communication	Examples
Declarative sentence	Statement	*John lives in Kent*
Interrogative sentence	Question	*Where were you born?*
Imperative sentence	Command	*Get up!*
Exclamatory sentence	Exclamation	*What a beauty she is!*

It is important to note, however, that there is no one-to-one correspondence between the grammatical form of a sentence and its function in communication (what is called its **illocutionary force**). This means that sentences with the same grammatical properties need not have the same illocutionary force and, conversely, that grammatically different sentences can have the same illocutionary force. Thus a request to put the car in the garage can be expressed in a variety of ways:

(212) Please put the car in the garage
(213) Could you put the car in the garage?
(214) Would you mind putting the car in the garage?
(215) You put the car in the garage?
(216) The car is still outside
(217) The car, John, please!

Additional examples are:

Grammatical form	Illocutionary force		Example
Declarative sentence	statement	(218)	I will be 40 next year
	command	(219)	You will leave this room at once
	request	(220)	I would love a martini
	warning	(221)	That plate is very hot
Interrogative sentence	question	(222)	Who is the President of the United States?
	request	(223)	Can you sing us a song?
	exclamation	(224)	Isn't that wonderful?
	command	(225)	What are you laughing at?
Imperative sentence	command	(226)	Shut up
	wish	(227)	Have a nice time
	invitation	(228)	Come and see us next week
	warning	(229)	Mind your head
Exclamatory sentence	exclamation	(230)	What a disappointment that book is!
	request	(231)	What lovely chocolates these are! (= Can I have another one?)

4.6 Sentences and the organization of the message

Sentences can convey messages in a variety of ways. Among the syntactic devices that play a role in the presentation of a message are **focus** and **wordorder**. Equally important in this connection are two sentence-types: **cleft sentences** and **pseudo-cleft sentences**.

4.6.1 *Focus*

English sentences normally have **end-focus**, which means that the last open-class item in the sentence is often the most prominent. This principle is illustrated in (232a), where *London* has end-focus:

(232) a. Robert is driving to LONDON

However, if the context requires this, it is possible to depart from the normal pattern by shifting the focus to other words. This is called **contrastive focus** and illustrated by examples (232b–d):

(232) b. Robert is driving TO London (not through London)
      c. Robert is DRIVING to London (not flying to London)
      d. ROBERT is driving to London (not Jack)

4.6.2 *Wordorder*

The second device, wordorder, involves a change in the linear order in which the words normally appear. The (a) examples below have the normal ('unmarked') order. The (b) examples have a 'marked' wordorder, that is certain parts of these sentences have been given emphasis by moving them to front-position. Cf:

(233) a. He lost his wife in the war
     b. His wife he lost in the war
(234) a. She was not a beauty
     b. A beauty she was not
(235) a. They are very keen on dances
     b. Dances they are very keen on
(236) a. It has not made him happy
     b. Happy it has not made him

4.6.3 *Cleft sentences and pseudo-cleft sentences*

A cleft sentence is a construction which makes it possible to put special emphasis on a particular constituent. This is done by 'cleaving' the sentence into two parts in such a way that the resulting sentence is of the pattern:

It + *be* + emphasized constituent + *who/that* . . .

Thus, corresponding to

(237) Peter posted this letter in New York last week

there are the following cleft analogues:

(237) a. It was *Peter* who posted this letter in New York last week
     b. It was *this letter* that Peter posted in New York last week
     c. It was *in New York* that Peter posted this letter last week
     d. It was *last week* that Peter posted this letter in New York

The emphasized constituents in (237a–d) function as subject, direct object and adverbial in the corresponding non-cleft sentence. Other constituents (indirect object, object attribute and predicator) are less frequently emphasized in this way, but we do find sentences like:

(238) It was *John* I lent my camera to
(239) It was *manager* that they appointed him
(240) It was *lecture* that Peter did in Beirut

The emphasized constituent may also be a clause, as in:

(241) It was *because he was abroad* that John could not be there

Note that in certain contexts it is possible to leave out the *that*-clause:

(242) Why could not John be there?
     It was because he was abroad (that John could not be there)

Sentences (243–246) seem to bear some resemblance to the type of elliptic cleft sentence that we have in (242):

(243) It's just that he is a fool
(244) It's only that I don't like him
(245) It's simply that she is a woman
(246) It's not that I don't want him here

Pseudo-cleft sentences, like cleft sentences, are used to give special emphasis to a particular part of the sentence. Pseudo-cleft sentences can be described as subject–predicator–subject attribute sentences, in which the subject is realized by a *what*-clause, the predicator by a form of *be* and the subject attribute by a noun phrase, an infinitive or an *-ing* participle. Examples:

(247) What killed him was alcohol
(248) What this University needs is a good Vice-Chancellor
(249) What he did was (to) write the address in his notebook
(250) What they are doing is spoiling their children

Other possible patterns are exemplified in the sentences below. They show that the *WH*-clause need not occur in sentence-initial position and that it may contain a *WH*-item other than *what*:

(251) A holiday in the sun is what I would like best
(252) This is where the robbers were shot by the police

Note that not all sentences introduced by a *what*-clause are pseudo-cleft. The sentences below show that only (253a) is a pseudo-cleft sentence, since it has a non-cleft paraphrase:

(253) a. What made him panic was an explosion
      b. An explosion made him panic
(254) a. What made him panic was a mystery to us
      b. *A mystery to us made him panic

Part Two

Structures

5. The structure of the word

English words minimally consist of one constituent, which is consequently a free morpheme.

Examples:

news	language	severe
paper	freeze	pupil
back	cylinder	starch
friend	grease	white

Words consisting of two or more constituents are formed by means of one of the two major word formation processes in English, affixation and compounding.

Affixation

Affixation is a process whereby a prefix or a suffix is added to a free morpheme (ie a root) or to a word that has already undergone a word formation rule.

This is illustrated in Table 5.1 (see p. 102). Note that affixation may entail changes in spelling and pronunciation.

It is useful to distinguish between root and base. The **root** of a word is that part which remains when all the affixes have been removed. Consequently, in each of the words in Table 5.1 *press* functions as the root. A **base** is any form to which an affix can be added, but not every base is a root. In Table 5.2, for example, the root *press* is also the base of *impress*, which, in turn, is the base of *impression*, etc.

The bottom line of Table 5.2 (see p. 102) shows that the word *un-impressionistic* consists of six constituent morphemes. The internal structure of the word, that is the way in which these constituents are related, is represented in Figure 5.1. Arrows point in the direction of bases:

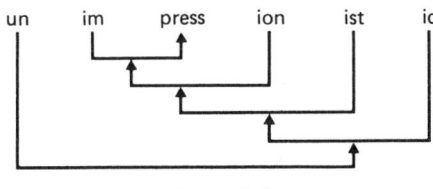

Figure 5.1

Table 5.1

Prefix	Prefix	Root	Suffix	Suffix	Suffix	Word
		press				press
		press	ed			pressed
		press	ing			pressing
	de	press				depress
	de	press	ing			depressing
	de	press	ive			depressive
		press	ure			pressure
		press	ur(e)	ize		pressurize
	de	press	ur(e)	ize		depressurize
	de	press	ur(e)	iz(e)	ation	depressurization
	com	press				compress
	ex	press				express
	op	press				oppress
	re	press				repress
	sup	press				suppress
	im	press				impress
	im	press	ive			impressive
	im	press	ive	ness		impressiveness
	im	press	ive	ly		impressively
	im	press	ion			impression
	im	press	ion	able		impressionable
	im	press	ion	ism		impressionism
	im	press	ion	ist		impressionist
	im	press	ion	ist	ic	impressionistic
un	im	press	ion	ist	ic	unimpressionistic

Table 5.2

		press			
	im	press			
	im	press	ion		
	im	press	ion	ist	
	im	press	ion	ist	ic
un	im	press	ion	ist	ic

Segmentation of words is not always as easy as examples like *unimpress-ionistic* might lead us to believe. In many English words the constituent morphemes do not follow each other in a linear order, as in the case of *unimpressionistic*. Examples are irregular forms like the plural of some nouns and the past tense of some verbs:

man	– men		take	– took
woman	– women		hit	– hit
foot	– feet		bring	– brought
mouse	– mice		go	– went

Words like *men* and *took* cannot easily be segmented into two distinct constituents. Nevertheless, on the basis of regular forms like *book-s* and *walk-ed* it is possible to analyse them as consisting of two morphemes, viz {*man*} + {s$_1$} and {*take*} + {ed$_1$}, respectively (where {ed$_1$} represents the past tense morpheme).

Compounding

Compounds are words such as *newspaper, paperback, watertight* and *duty-free*. As Table 5.3 shows, compounds are formed in a variety of ways. Orthographic practice varies a great deal, since compounds may be hyphenated, written as one word or as separate words. The examples show that compounds are not necessarily combinations of free morphemes (as in *newspaper*), but include cases where a free morpheme combines with an affixed word (as in *hard-hitting*).

Table 5.3

	Noun	Adjective	Verb	Adverb
Noun	daylight wineglass life insurance car park	watertight duty-free blood red garden-fresh	gatecrash breathtaking handmade airborne	passer-by looker-on
Adjective	greenhouse blackboard madman heavyweight	red-hot icy-cold bitter-sweet shabby-genteel	good-looking easy-going slow-running deepfreeze	
Verb	pickpocket chewing gum searchlight watchdog		hearsay make-believe would-be	takeover hold-up lay-by know-how
Adverb	overcoat counter-attack underworld afterthought	wide awake evergreen mock-heroic oversensitive	ill-treat underestimate hard-hitting well-read	henceforth

6. The structure of the phrase

6.1 The noun phrase

In the structure of the noun phrase we can distinguish three functions: head, determiner and modifier.

The head of a noun phrase is usually realized by a noun or pronoun, as in:

Books are getting more and more expensive
We are running out of *sugar*
Smith is extremely difficult to get on with
Who appointed *them*?
They prefer *mine* to *yours*
His parents are dead
My father has bought *a very expensive car*
The police have arrested *the man who married John's sister*

The first five examples show that, if the noun phrase consists of a head only, the head must be realized by a plural count noun, a mass noun, a proper noun or a pronoun.

The head of a noun phrase may also be realized by an adjective (in which case it is usually introduced by the definite article and often has generic reference), by a participle or by a numeral:

the poor   the impossible   the unknown the wounded and the dying
the rich   the inevitable   the accused   these two
the English   the supernatural the deceased all three

Finally we find noun phrases whose head is realized by a noun in the genitive or by a genitive-like noun in which the apostrophe is dropped. The traditional label for this type of genitive is 'local genitive'. Examples:

I am staying at my *aunt's*
The *grocer's* is at the corner of the street
Harrods is in Knightsbridge
There is a *Boots* in the High Street

Such cases should be distinguished from the genitives in the following noun phrases in which the head has been ellipted and is recoverable from the context:

Our garden is larger than *your neighbour's*
Mary's is an interesting essay as well
That typewriter is *O'Neil's*

In subsections 6.1.1–6.1.4 we shall be dealing with the various ways in which the other two functions in the structure of the noun phrase (determiner and modifier) can be realized. As appears from the two examples below, the function modifier may be realized by (a) constituent(s) preceding the head (premodifier), (a) constituent(s) following the head (postmodifier) and by an 'interrupted' constituent on either side of the head (discontinuous modifier):

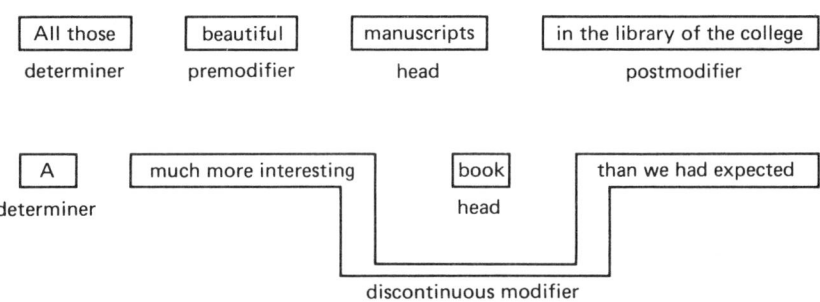

6.1.1 *Determiner*

The function determiner can be realized by a wide range of items, such as the definite article, the indefinite article, possessive pronouns, demonstrative pronouns, numerals, etc. These items occur in a fixed order with respect to each other. Cf. for example:

> all his children
>   his three children

where *all* must precede *his*, which, in turn, must precede *three*. Consequently it is useful to distinguish three determiner sub-functions: **predeterminer**, **central determiner** and **postdeterminer**. The (classes of) items that can realize each of these sub-functions are listed in Table 6.1.

Table 6.1 should not be interpreted as implying that there are no restrictions on the selection of items from each of the columns. The choice of a given item from one column may impose certain restrictions on the selection of items from other columns. It is obvious, for example, that the choice of *many* as predeterminer necessitates the choice of the indefinite article (which must be followed by a singular head). Similarly the word *own* as postdeterminer must be preceded by a genitive or a possessive pronoun. Some of the co-occurrence restrictions that obtain in noun phrases are dealt with below.

Table 6.1

FUNCTION	Determiner		
	Predeterminer	Central determiner	Postdeterminer
REALIZATION	*all* *both* *double* *half* *twice* *many* (*a*) *such* (*a*) *what* (*a*)	definite article indefinite article demonstrative pronouns possessive pronouns specifying genitive *another* *any* *each* *either* *enough* *every* *much* *neither* *no* *some* *what* *which* *whose*	cardinal numbers ordinal numbers *next, last* *few, fewer, fewest* *little, less, least* *many, more, most* *other* *own* *same* *such*

Predeterminer

The items *all*, *double*, *half* and *twice* can combine with both singular and plural heads:

all poetry
all these expensive school uniforms
double Peter's salary
double these high amounts
half this cheese
half Britain's natural resources
twice his not inconsiderable energy
twice these sums

Both, on the other hand, requires a plural head:

both my sisters
both his last two newspaper articles

Of the above items *half* is the only one that can be followed by the indefinite article:

half an hour

Many, *such* and *what*, when realizing the predeterminer function, are obligatorily followed by the indefinite article:

many a time
such a disgrace
what a pity

Central determiner

The definite article, the demonstrative and possessive pronouns, and the specifying genitive are alike in that they can be preceded by the predeterminer items *all*, *both*, *double*, *half* and *twice*, and followed by cardinal numbers, ordinal numbers and the words *last* and *next*. They also collocate with most of the other postdeterminer items. The indefinite article can be preceded by *half*, *many*, *such* and *what*. Examples:

double the amount	his many grievances
the fourth chapter	the most mistakes
both these books	Jim's other car
this last question	these few exceptions
half their property	half a minute
our next attempt	
all Peter's clothes	
Jennifer's third baby	

The other items listed in the second column of Table 6.1 (*another . . . whose*) cannot, as a rule, be preceded by predeterminer items. Examples:

another beautiful day	neither side
any other solution	no problems
each third sentence	some Japanese drawings
either case	what friends
enough intelligent students	which university
every English grammar	whose books
much useful information	

In general central determiner items are mutually exclusive, so that the following noun phrases are unacceptable:

*the my brother	*this each case
*John's these essays	*my any books

An exception is the combination of *every* with a possessive, as in

his (John's, whose) every wish

Postdeterminer

Postdeterminer items exhibit such a wide range of collocational possibilities and restrictions that it is very hard to formulate general rules governing their behaviour. We therefore prefer to illustrate their use by means of some examples:

half his many books	every other week
any other day	any more books
Maigret's last case	what little money (he had)
the first two pages	what few friends (he had)
no other chance	my own car
the same man	some more sugar

Not all postdeterminer items are mutally exclusive. Consider, for example:

one more drink	few other people	the last two weeks
little more news	little other information	the next few years
many more accidents	many other problems	the first ten arrivals

Note that when postdeterminer items co-occur their order is usually fixed. However, there are exceptions, as appears from the following pair:

the other three men
the three other men

The status of the item *such* is problematic. It may be looked upon as a predeterminer item when followed by the indefinite article. However, it may also be classed as a postdeterminer item, since it may be preceded by some central determiner items and co-occurs with some postdeterminer items. Consider:

any such questions   few such candidates
no such nonsense   two such blunders
some such concept   many such incidents

6.1.2 *Premodifier*

In the structure of the noun phrase the function premodifier may be realized by means of:

1. an adjective phrase
2. a noun phrase
3. a classifying genitive
4. an adverb phrase

Adjective phrase

The choice of an adjective phrase (or adjective phrases) in the structure of a noun phrase is independent of previous choices from the predeterminer, central determiner or postdeterminer items. In other words, all the examples given so far could be expanded by adding one or more adjective phrases:

all poetry   – all English poetry
both my sisters   – both my younger sisters
half this cheese   – half this French cheese
our next attempt   – our next abortive attempt
any other solution – any other acceptable solution

In the above examples the premodifier is realized by one-word adjective phrases. The following examples show that the adjective phrase may also contain an intensifier:

a very old lady   this rather expensive clock
an extremely difficult problem his incredibly stupid behaviour

In principle there are no restrictions on the number of adjectives that may occur before the head. What is important, however, is that the order in which adjectives appear is not always free. To a large extent the order in adjectival strings would seem to be determined by the semantic class to which the adjectives belong. It is possible to distinguish a large number of semantic classes, but we shall here confine ourselves to adjectives whose positional behaviour shows some regularity. We shall distinguish:

1. adjectives denoting nationality : *English, Chinese, Dutch, Swiss . . .*
2. adjectives denoting substance : *silk, wooden, woollen . . .*
3. adjectives denoting colour : *red, green, violet . . .*
4. adjectives denoting age : *old, young . . .*
5. adjectives denoting shape : *round, rectangular, square . . .*
6. adjectives denoting size : *large, huge, small, big . . .*
7. adjectives denoting properties other than those mentioned under 1–6 : *expensive, gay, fine, secret, brave, silent, angry, obscure, dirty . . .*

Class 1 adjectives appear immediately before the head of the noun phrase, class 2 adjectives precede class 1 adjectives, etc. Examples are shown in Table 6.2.

Table 6.2

Det.	7	6	5	4	3	2	1	Head
an	expensive						Swiss	watch
that		small	round					table
John's					red	woollen		sweater
a	brave			young			Dutch	hero
some		big			grey			buildings
				old			French	wine
an	ugly		square			wooden		box
his		huge		old	black		American	car
	lovely				blue		English	pottery
a			rectangular			plastic		tray

Note that on the whole adjectives can only be coordinated if they belong to the same semantic class. Compare:

a clever but ugly girl   – *a clever but Swiss girl
a beautiful and fast car   – *a beautiful and red car
a sad and moving tale   – *a sad and old tale
a kind and intelligent boy – *a kind and young boy

Apart from 'pure' adjectives we also find -*ing* participles and -*ed* participles as premodifiers in the noun phrase. Not all of these participles are fully adjectival in character, as appears from the fact that some, like many 'pure' adjectives, can be modified by *very*, whereas others cannot. Some examples are given in Table 6.3.

Adjective phrases do not always follow items realizing the determiner function. This deviation from normal wordorder, which may be called

Table 6.3

	very	**very*
-ing participle	a sweeping statement an interesting proposition a fascinating novel a trying experience a revolting man	barking dogs playing children a passing car the rising sun moving shadows
-ed participle	a mixed company a respected businessman an involved style isolated villages irritated remarks	an escaped prisoner the vanished jewels a fallen angel a divorced couple a born leader

'shifted premodification', occurs in noun phrases containing the indefinite article as central determiner under either of the following conditions:

1. the adjective phrase contains one of the following intensifying adverbs: *as, so, how, however, ever so, that, this, too, enough, more* and *less*;
2. the head of the adjective phrase is in the comparative degree and preceded by *no, much* and *far*.

Examples:

> how strange a story
> however brave a soldier
> ever so slight a foreign accent
> too hot a day
> no worse a plan
> far cheaper a method

Note that in some cases there are alternative constructions, in others there are not. Compare:

> far cheaper a method –   a far cheaper method
> how strange a story   – *a how strange story

Noun phrase

The head of a noun phrase can be premodified by another noun phrase, which often consists of a head only. Many of such combinations are fixed and it is often hard, if not impossible, to distinguish them from compound nouns. Examples:

sign language	government decision
weather chart	Yorkshire moors
garden city	student protest
church bazaar	traffic jam
London policemen	film critic
language disorder	transistor radio
tax evasion	speed limit

circus act
chess competition
diary entry
car battery
sports review
programme guide

laboratory test
frequency count
patrol car
sex maniac
news summary
radio theatre

It is not uncommon for the noun phrase head to be premodified by a noun phrase which, in turn, is premodified by another noun phrase. Consider, for example

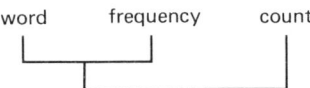

Other examples are:

London street guide
police patrol car
language disorder studies

transistor radio batteries
stock market report
car export figures

Cambridge University Press

the 1975 Reith lecture programme
BBC World Service listeners
The University of Edinburgh Psychology Department
The Brian Matthew request show
Social Science Research Council grants
London County Council Education Committee
the Schools Council Primary School Modern Languages Programme

It is also possible for the noun phrase head to be premodified by coordinated nouns:

a Punch and Judy show
world and U.K. reports
a blood and thunder story
cheese and cucumber sandwiches

a bread and butter letter
the Eric Morecambe and Ernie Wise Show
a milk and fruit diet
A Jekyll and Hyde personality

Classifying genitive

As the following examples show, the noun phrase head may be premodified by a noun in the genitive:

a dog's life
child's play
a doctor's degree

a ladies' man
a men's shop
women's rights

Note that this (**classifying**) genitive is different from the (**specifying**) genitive that functions as central determiner. The latter type may be separated from the head noun by an adjective. Compare:

John's expensive shirt – *a men's expensive shop

The word preceding a specifying genitive qualifies the genitive, not the head noun; on the other hand, it is the head noun which is qualified when the genitive is classifying. Compare:

That genitives can have different functions in the structure of the noun phrase appears from an example like the following, where the first genitive is specifying, the second classifying:

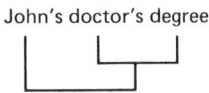

Adverb phrase

Finally the noun phrase head can be premodified by an adverb phrase which consists of a head only. Examples:

the then chairman   an up train
an away game   a through road

6.1.3 *Postmodifier*

In the structure of the noun phrase the function postmodifier may be realized by means of:

1. an adjective phrase
2. an adverb phrase
3. a prepositional phrase
4. a noun phrase
5. a finite clause
6. a non-finite clause

Adjective phrase

Adjective phrases may follow the noun head in the following cases:

(a) When noun head and adjective form an idiomatic expression:

Lords spiritual	Solicitor General	the sum total
Lords temporal	court martial	the amount due
heir apparent	(from) time immemorial	
Attorney General	China proper	

(b) When the postmodifying adjective is one of a limited number of items, including *present*, *alive*, *involved*, *concerned* and a few adjectives in *-able/-ible*:

> the people present (= who were present)
> the happiest man alive the greatest difficulty imaginable
> the information available the only persons responsible
> the factors involved the easiest solution conceivable
> all people concerned

(c) When the noun phrase head is a pronoun:

> something interesting somebody important
> nothing useful anything original

(d) When the adjective is followed by a prepositional phrase:

> people averse to hard work
> the difficulties implicit in this kind of undertaking
> boys interested in bird-watching
> a wallpaper similar to yours
> a house different from Peter's

(e) When the adjective is followed by an infinitive clause. The adjective may be preceded by *too* or followed by *enough* (in some cases obligatorily so):

> a theory (too) difficult to a man easy to persuade
> explain a chest too heavy to move
> children reluctant to obey a project too expensive to
> books hard to come by finance
> soldiers eager (enough) to go a man wealthy enough to foot
> on leave the bill
> customers unwilling to pay students clever enough to
> understand this

(f) When the adjective is in the comparative degree or preceded by *as*, *more* or *less*, and followed by a clause of comparison (full or reduced):

> a car faster than your Jaguar
> a room bigger than he had imagined
> a country-house more expensive than John's
> a plan less ambitious than we expected

> an office-block as tall as the Empire State Building
> a man as rich as my father
> a girl as dim as her sister is clever
> a performance as good as I have ever seen

(g) When the adjective is preceded by *so*, and followed by a finite or non-finite clause:

> a point so trivial that it is not worth mentioning
> a cave so dark that we could not see a thing
> a light so intense as to blind the eyes
> a valley so beautiful as to defy description

Adverb phrase

The following are examples of noun phrases with heads postmodified by an adverb phrase:

the way down	the man outside
the way in	this point here
the way up	the car over there
the way back	the people out there
the journey up	the air up here
the journey down	living conditions down there
the road ahead	the day before

Prepositional phrase

Noun phrase heads may be postmodified by a prepositional phrase, as in:

the city of Rome	the edge of the desk
a pound of sugar	A Grammar of Contemporary English
friends of mine	the path along the canal
a house of my father's	the day before yesterday
the idea of it	the hope of reaching the semi-finals
the book on top	objections to Britain joining the Common Market
the restaurant opposite Harrods	the problem of how much to spend next year
the trees in the park	speculations about how he acquired his fortune

Noun phrases may contain two or more prepositional phrases:

> the book on archaeology by Professor Smith
> the house at the corner of the street
> the flowers in the vase on the table
> the year before the election of Nixon in the U.S.
> the theft of the documents in the safe of his office in Berkeley Square
> the story of the accident at the funfair in Battersea Park

In the above examples the syntactic structure is not always the same. Thus in the first example the second prepositional phrase modifies all that precedes:

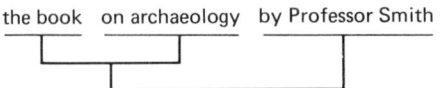

whereas in the second example the second prepositional phrase modifies only the NP of the first:

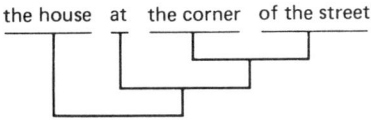

Noun phrase

Postmodification by means of noun phrases is rare. Examples:

girls your age   a car that colour
a rock that shape   a hat this size

Finite clause

Three types of finite clause can be used as postmodifier: relative clauses, appositive clauses and clauses introduced by temporal conjunctions. **Relative clauses** are introduced by relative pronouns, **appositive clauses** by the conjunction *that* or by *WH*-words.

Relative clauses

It is necessary to distinguish two types of relative clause: **restrictive** and **non-restrictive**. The former supply information that is essential for the identification of the antecedent; the latter contain information that is not strictly required to identify the antecedent. Non-restrictive clauses are therefore usually omissible. Another difference is that restrictive clauses follow the antecedent without a break in the intonation pattern, whereas non-restrictive ones are clearly separated from the antecedent intonationally and are enclosed within commas in writing.

The pronoun *that* can only be used in restrictive clauses, which are also characterized by the fact that they may be non-introduced when the relative pronoun does not function as the subject of the relative clause. Clauses with unstressed *there* are non-introduced as well.

Restrictive:

Is he the man whose house was burnt down?
This is the best book that has been written on the subject recently
This is the best book he has written on the subject
Is he the man you were followed by?
Christopher is no longer the man he used to be
This is the best book there is on the subject

Non-restrictive:

There were two passengers in the taxi, who were killed
John, whose wife left him last week, feels quite relieved
Eliot, whom he had always greatly admired, paid him a visit one day
They moved to Paris, which had always fascinated them

Appositive clauses

We can distinguish two types of appositive clause: those introduced by *WH*-words and those introduced by *that*:

the issue who should be the leader
the problem how this could be solved
our hesitation whether we ought to go

the hope that these negotiations would be a success
the fact that there is an enormous deficit
the news that he had been fired

The difference between appositive clauses and relative clauses appears from the fact that noun phrases containing the former allow paraphrases containing the copula *be*, whereas noun phrases containing the latter do not:

Appositive:

the news that he is ill	:	The news is that he is ill
the question whether we should ask him	:	The question is whether we should ask him

Relative:

the news that we heard over the radio	:	*The news is that we heard over the radio
the question which we should ask him	:	*The question is which we should ask him

It is not always easy to distinguish between appositive *that*-clauses and relative *that*-clauses. They differ in the following respects:

(a) *that* in appositive clauses is a conjunction which cannot be omitted;
(b) *that* in relative clauses is a pronoun which, under certain conditions, can be omitted and which, depending on the antecedent noun, can usually be replaced by either *who* or *which*;
(c) unlike relative *that*, which functions as subject, object, etc, appositive *that* has no such function in the structure of the clause it introduces;

(d) whereas there are no restrictions on the antecedent nouns of relative clauses, the noun preceding an appositive clause can only be an abstract noun like *fact*, *news*, *claim*, *rumour*, *suggestion*, etc.

Clauses introduced by temporal conjunctions

The third type of finite clause that can function as postmodifier in the noun phrase is introduced by temporal conjunctions such as *before*, *after*, *since*, etc.:

the days before he died   the time since he has been chairman
the years after she was born the lonely hours until help arrived

Non-finite clause

Three types of non-finite clause can occur in postmodification: infinitive clauses, *-ing* participle clauses and *-ed* participle clauses. As the examples show, some infinitive clauses are reduced relative or appositive clauses. *-Ing* participle and *-ed* participle clauses are reduced relative clauses.

Infinitive clauses

The infinitive in these clauses is always preceded by *to*:

He is the man to talk to
John lacks the energy to write such a book
They were the first men to land on the moon
Peter's was the second car to reach the finish
What are the conclusions to be drawn?
These are the factors to be taken into account
Is he the man with whom to do business?
The Adelphi is the hotel at which to stay
Peter's wish to be buried in England could not be fulfilled
Our hope to reach the semi-finals was unfounded
The question whether to join now or later is irrelevant
The decision when to leave will be taken tomorrow
We have no indication where to look

If the clause has an overt subject, it is introduced by *for*:

There is no cause for her to be so upset
Dr Mann is the gynaecologist for Mary to see
That is the course for you to attend
I think I have found the style for her to imitate
What was the reason for her to think that John is dishonest?

-ing participle clauses

Students wishing to take the examination before June should contact the secretary

The gold was discovered by three men digging a shaft
I received a letter asking me to return to England
What is the deep structure underlying this sentence?
This happened in the week following our visit to the British Museum
They regularly publish articles describing the effect of air pollution on
    people's health
The work being done on this subject at Harvard is of the utmost
    importance
The point being made here may seem to be trivial

-ed participle clauses

Soldiers found guilty of looting will be shot
None of the children injured in the accident were taken to hospital
The general impression given by this book is favourable
The techniques used by the research team are sound
The candidates selected all have a very high IQ
This is the result of the attention paid to this problem during the last few
    decades
The evidence adduced for his hypothesis is inconclusive

6.1.4 *Discontinuous modifier*

We shall here exemplify structures in which part of the modifier precedes
the noun head, the rest following it in postmodification. We distinguish the
following cases, which, as the examples show, also allow alternative
constructions with postmodification only:

1. adjective + noun + prepositional phrase:

   a similar wallpaper to yours   – a wallpaper similar to yours
   a different house from Peter's   – a house different from Peter's

2. adjective + noun + infinitive clause:

   a difficult theory to explain   – a theory difficult to explain
   an easy man to persuade   – a man easy to persuade

3. comparative adjective + noun + *than* + (reduced) comparative clause
   or noun phrase:

   a faster car than your Jaguar   – a car faster than your Jaguar
   a richer man than his father   – a man richer than his father
       used to be   used to be
   a longer distance than 5 miles   – a distance longer than 5 miles

4. *as* + adjective + noun + *as* + (reduced) comparative clause:

   as rich a man as my father   – a man as rich as my father
   as intelligent a man as I would   – a man as intelligent as I would
       like to be   like to be

5. *so* + adjective + noun + *that*-clause or *as to*-clause:

so dark a cave that we could not see a thing	– a cave so dark that we could not see a thing
so intense a light as to blind the eyes	– a light so intense as to blind the eyes

6. *too* + adjective + noun + infinitive clause:

too heavy a chest to move	– a chest too heavy to move
too expensive a project to finance	– a project too expensive to finance

6.2 The adjective phrase

In the structure of the adjective phrase we can distinguish two functions: head and modifier.

The head of an adjective phrase is usually realized by an adjective . The function modifier may be realized by a constituent preceding the head (premodifier), by a constituent following the head (postmodifier) and by an 'interrupted' constituent on either side of the head (discontinuous modifier).

6.2.1 *Premodifier*

The function premodifier is realized by adverb phrases:

very useful	so utterly banal
extremely difficult	far more interesting
fairly easy	quite exceptionally brave
surprisingly honest	hardly more clean

6.2.2 *Postmodifier*

The function postmodifier in adjective phrases may be realized by:

1. the adverb *enough*
2. a prepositional phrase
3. a finite clause
4. a non-finite clause

Enough

The only adverb that can postmodify an adjectival head is *enough*. Note that *enough* may be followed by an infinitive clause:

clever enough
quick enough to be in time

Prepositional phrase

The following are examples of adjective phrases postmodified by a prepositional phrase. Note that some adjectives such as *averse* and *fond* require
postmodification. In other cases postmodification is optional.

afraid of mice	capable of murder
good at bridge	full of water
glad of a change	furious with her friend
loyal to one's principles	green with envy
averse to hard work	fond of going to the cinema
qualified for the job	worried about what would happen next

Finite clause

Clausal postmodification of adjectival heads is usually realized by *that*-
clauses:

I am very worried that he might come to grief
We were surprised that he should have turned up at all
Henry should be grateful that he is still alive
I am glad that you can come
Were you afraid that he might not finish in time?
The headmaster was disappointed that Mary got only two A-levels
Are you certain that Phil is married?
Chrissy was mad that we had left without her

Clauses postmodifying adjectival heads may also be introduced by *WH*-
words (or by *if*):

I am doubtful whether (if) I should go
He is not sure who did it
I was not aware how shocked he was at my refusal

After comparative adjectives in *-er* the finite clause is introduced by *than*:

The trip was longer than we had thought
Jim is prouder than his brother was

Note that for the last example there is an alternative construction with a
reduced comparative clause:

Jim is prouder than his brother

A comparison of the two sentences below

This bridge is longer than Chelsea bridge
This bridge is longer than two miles

shows that only the first sentence can be looked upon as an example of a
reduced comparative clause since we have

This bridge is longer than Chelsea bridge is

but not

*This bridge is longer than two miles are

Non-finite clause

The adjectival head can be followed by an infinitive clause:

afraid to go	eager to please
anxious to leave	delighted to come
apt to make mistakes	inclined to believe gossip
interested to hear about it	willing to get up early
hesitant to answer questions	pleased to meet your friend
liable to be punished	proud to be chosen

The infinitive clause may be introduced by a *WH*-word:

I feel dubious what to do next
Why are you so hesitant whether to invite him or not?
She feels uncertain what to tell her husband

If the infinitive clause has an overt subject, it is introduced by *for*:

I am quite willing for this plan to be submitted
The children were very eager for the party to start
I shall be sorry for Esther to leave us
The Town Council would be prepared for the refugees to be housed in
   that new block of flats

The adjectives *worth* and *busy* are followed by an *-ing* participle clause:

This problem is worth looking into
They were busy packing

6.2.3 *Discontinuous modifier*

The following four cases can be distinguished:

1. *so* + adjective + *that*-clause or *as to*-clause:

It was so hot that I could not sleep
This exercise is so difficult that only the best students can do it
His latest film is so brilliant as to excite even the most jaded filmgoer
The price of that book is so high as to be prohibitive

2. *as* + adjective + *as* + (reduced) comparative clause or noun phrase:

She is as pretty as her sister
Peter is as cruel as he is intelligent
The trip was as expensive as we had expected
It is as far as ten miles
It weighs as heavy as ten pounds

Note that after *not* we find both *as* and *so*:

The President's speeches are not as (so) predictable as they used to be

3. *more/less* + adjective + *than* + (reduced) comparative clause or noun phrase:

> He is definitely more balanced than his father
> Brian's proposal was less attractive than the one David made last
>   week
> Fellini's film is less interesting than Bergman's
> The shops were more crowded than they were on Christmas Eve
> My present was less expensive than £10

4. *too* + adjective + infinitive clause:

> Surely, he is too old to be her husband
> Sara's handwriting is too spidery to be legible
> It is too hot for the children to play in the garden
> His campaign is too expensive for the party to finance it

6.3 The adverb phrase

In the structure of the adverb phrase we can distinguish two functions: head and modifier.

The head of an adverb phrase is realized by an adverb. The function modifier may be realized by a constituent preceding the head (premodifier), by a constituent following the head (postmodifier) and by an 'interrupted' constituent on either side of the head (discontinuous modifier). It should be noted that adverb phrases with postmodification only are rare. On the other hand, heads of adverb phrases are regularly modified by discontinuous modifiers, just like adjectival heads.

6.3.1 *Premodifier*

The premodifier of the adverb phrase head can only be realized by intensifying adverb phrases:

very seldom	extremely stupidly
perfectly well	fairly often
rather foolishly	exceptionally quickly
too optimistically	quite soon
much more carefully	hardly less cruelly

6.3.2 *Postmodifier*

The postmodifier in adverb phrases may be realized by:

1. the adverb *enough*
2. a finite clause (after comparative adverbs in *-er*)

Enough

Adverbial heads can be postmodified by the adverb *enough*, which, as in the case of adjectival postmodification, can be followed by an infinitive clause:

well enough
bravely enough to deserve a medal

Finite clause

Comparative adverbs in *-er* can be postmodified by finite clauses introduced by *than*:

These students work harder than we had expected
The train left earlier than the stationmaster had told us

Of the following two examples the first can be looked upon as a reduced comparative clause, the second cannot:

Caroline arrived later than my brother
Caroline arrived later than five o'clock

since we have

Caroline arrived later than my brother did

but not

*Caroline arrived later than five o'clock did

6.3.3 *Discontinuous modifier*

Adverbial heads, like adjectival ones, may be modified by discontinuous structures. Again we distinguish four cases:

1. *so* + adverb + *that*-clause or *as to*-clause:

   They worked so hard that they finished before five
   The children were treated so cruelly that they still have nightmares
   He spoke so eloquently as to convince everyone
   Marcus behaves so irresponsibly as to endanger the whole project

2. *as* + adverb + *as* + (reduced) comparative clause or noun phrase:

   He loves her as much as he did 25 years ago
   We need your support as badly as you need ours
   My dog runs as fast as yours
   He speaks Russian as fluently as a native
   The book was published as recently as last week

3. *more/less* + adverb + *than* + (reduced) comparative clause or noun phrase:

   The boy participates more actively than we had expected
   These problems are treated less theoretically than they usually are
   He reacted less kindly than yesterday

This sort of accident seems to occur more frequently than in the past
That train used to run more often than every two hours

4. *too* + adverb + infinitive clause

We are travelling too slowly to get there by noon
He spoke too flippantly to be taken seriously
The boy was running too fast for the policeman to overtake him
He offered his services too eagerly for us to accept them without
    misgiving

6.4 The verb phrase

The verb phrase consists of verbal forms only, except in the case of
multi-word verbs. The maximum number of verbal forms is five. The
principal part of the verb phrase is the lexical (or main) verb. The lexical
verb can occur on its own, but it may co-occur with auxiliary verbs in
patterns of varying degrees of complexity:

Lexical verb + one auxiliary

When a lexical verb (LV) co-occurs with one auxiliary verb, we have the
following possibilities:

1. LV + modal auxiliary   : John *can write*
2. LV + auxiliary of periphrasis (*do*)   : *Does* John *write?*
                                                         John *does* not *write*
3. LV + auxiliary of emphasis (*do*)   : *Do write* quicker!
                                                         He *does write* quicker
4. LV + auxiliary of the perfective aspect
   (*have*)   : John *has written*
5. LV + auxiliary of the progressive aspect
   (*be*)   : John *is writing*
6. LV + auxiliary of the passive voice (*be*)   : The letter *was*
                                                         written by John

Do as an auxiliary of periphrasis and of emphasis is found in verb phrases
that contain maximally two verbal forms. In other words, verb phrases
containing the auxiliary *do* cannot contain a modal auxiliary nor an
auxiliary of the perfective aspect, the progressive aspect or the passive
voice. Negative imperatives (like *Don't be taken in*) are an exception.

Lexical verb + two (or more) auxiliaries

When a verb phrase contains more than one auxiliary, it can range in
complexity from three to (maximally) five verbal forms:

Two auxiliaries:
<pre>
may have written
may be   writing
may be   written
has been writing
has been written
is   being written
</pre>

Three auxiliaries:
<pre>
may have been writing
may have been written
may be   being written
has been being written
</pre>

Four auxiliaries: may have been being written (rare)

It should be noted that the categories of the perfective aspect, the progressive aspect and the passive voice are realized by means of an auxiliary verb and a suffix:

perfective aspect : *have* + *-ed* participle suffix: *have* writt *-en*
progressive aspect: *be*   + *-ing* participle suffix: *be*   writ *-ing*
passive voice   : *be*   + *-ed* participle suffix: *be*   writt *-en*

In verb phrases containing a combination of these categories the suffix is invariably attached to the verb immediately following the auxiliary which, together with the suffix, realizes the category in question. This can be illustrated as follows:

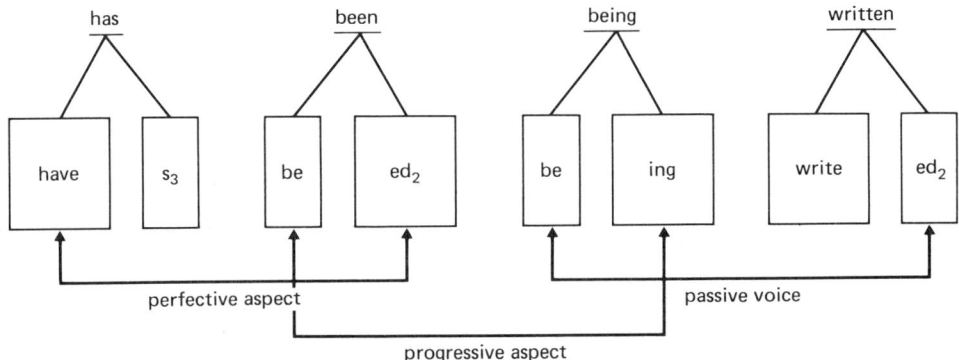

The co-occurrence patterns in the English verb phrase are set out in Table 6.4.

6.5 The prepositional phrase

In the structure of the prepositional phrase two functions can be distinguished: prepositional and prepositional complement.

The function prepositional is usually realized by a preposition alone (simple or complex).

Table 6.4

Modal	Perfec-tive	Pro-gressive	Passive	Peri/Emph.	LV	Examples
					+	writes
				+	+	does write
			+		+	is written
		+			+	is writing
	+				+	has written
+					+	may write
+	+				+	may have written
	+	+			+	has been writing
		+	+		+	is being written
+		+			+	may be writing
+			+		+	may be written
	+		+		+	has been written
+	+	+			+	may have been writing
+	+		+		+	may have been written
	+	+	+		+	has been being written
+		+	+		+	may be being written
+	+	+	+		+	may have been being written

Examples:

on the roof
until next week

on account of the rain
in terms of money

A prepositional phrase can be modified by an intensifying adverb as well as by a noun phrase.

Examples:

right behind the house
partly because of his parents
exactly like your father
reasonably near the office

two weeks before his death
some time after the election
a mile from the city centre
ten yards behind the house

In the above examples the prepositional complement is realized by noun phrases. There are four other possibilities: a *WH*-clause, an *-ing* participle clause, a prepositional phrase (rare) and an adverb phrase (rare):

I was astonished at what he said
We are satisfied with where we live
You irritate me by talking like that
We were late through John having mislaid his car keys
The baby crawled from under the table
Until quite recently he lived in London

The analysis of the following cases is problematic. They may either be looked upon as prepositional phrases modified by an adverb or as adverb phrases with a prepositional phrase in postmodification:

up at the farm
back in the summer

down by the river
down at the bus stop

7. The structure of the sentence: Functions

7.1 Introductory

Sentences can be described in two ways: a **functional description** specifies what **functions** their constituents have in sentence structure, a **categorial description** gives information about the **categories** to which their constituents belong. We shall see below that an adequate description combines both kinds of information.

Sentence constituents can have the following functions, all of which will be defined below:

Subject (Su)

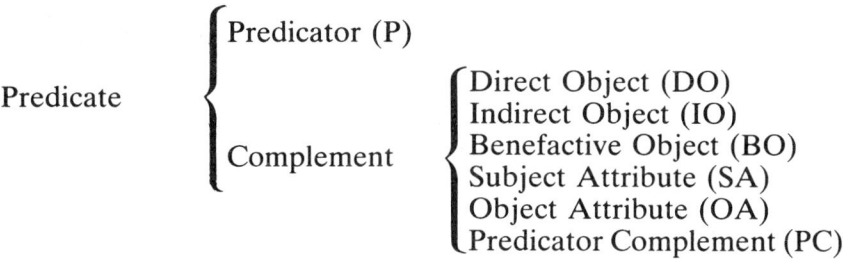

Adverbial (A)

The terms subject, predicate and adverbial are function-labels denoting the relation between the constituents bearing these labels and the sentence as a whole. In other words they are function-labels for immediate constituents of the sentence. The terms predicator and complement (of which there are six types) are function-labels denoting the relation between the constituents bearing these labels and a subpart of the sentence, viz that part which functions as predicate. These relations are illustrated in Figure 7.1.

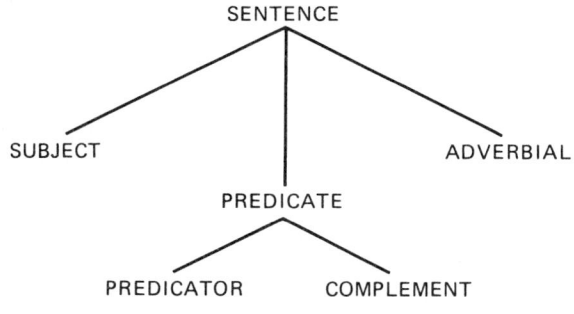

Figure 7.1

127

In terms of the functions that their constituents have in sentential structure examples (1–12) below can be described as follows. The intermediate labels 'predicate' and 'complement' have been omitted.

(1) The moon – rose	: Su–P
(2) Many students – enjoyed – the concert	: Su–P–DO
(3) That problem – seems – easy	: Su–P–SA
(4) He – has – two cars	: Su–P–PC
(5) Mary – works – in London	: Su–P–A
(6) She – sings – well	: Su–P–A
(7) The firm – has offered – Jim – a job	: Su–P–IO–DO
(8) Frank – left – his wife – last week	: Su–P–DO–A
(9) Joan – will make – her husband – very happy	: Su–P–DO–OA
(10) This street – reminds – me – of Paris	: Su–P–DO–PC
(11) My boss – has bought – his daughter – a flat	: Su–P–BO–DO
(12) We – met – the Joneses – unexpectedly – in New York – last year	: Su–P–DO–A–A–A

In these sentences all the noun phrases in initial position function as subject, all the verb phrases as predicator. Constituents that follow the verb phrase can have a variety of functions.

Sentences can also be described in categorial terms, that is in terms of the phrases of which they are made up. A categorial description of sentences (1–12) looks as follows:

(1) The moon – rose	: NP–VP
(2) Many students – enjoyed – the concert	: NP–VP–NP
(3) That problem – seems – easy	: NP–VP–Adj.P
(4) He – has – two cars	: NP–VP–NP
(5) Mary – works – in London	: NP–VP–Prep.P
(6) She – sings – well	: NP–VP–Adv.P
(7) The firm – has offered – Jim – a job	: NP–VP–NP–NP
(8) Frank – left – his wife – last week	: NP–VP–NP–NP
(9) Joan – will make – her husband – very happy	: NP–VP–NP–Adj.P
(10) This street – reminds – me – of Paris	: NP–VP–NP–Prep.P
(11) My boss – has bought – his daughter – a flat	: NP–VP–NP–NP
(12) We – met – the Joneses – unexpectedly – in New York – last year	: NP–VP–NP–Adv.P Prep.P–NP

A description of a sentence in terms of its constituent phrases is obviously inadequate. For example, sentences (7), (8) and (11) consist of identical strings of phrases (NP–VP–NP–NP). That they are nevertheless different appears from the fact that (7a) is a possible paraphrase of (7), but that (8a) and (11a) are ungrammatical:

(7)a.   The firm has offered a job to Jim
(8)a.   *Frank left last week to his wife
(11)a. *My boss has bought a flat to his daughter

This means that in addition to describing a sentence formally as a string of phrases we must also specify what function each phrase has.

As we have already demonstrated in the case of sentences (7), (8) and (11), there is no one-to-one correspondence between categorial and functional representations of sentences. In other words, it is possible to give the same categorial description to sentences which are otherwise different. Similarly, the same functional representation can be given to sentences which differ with respect to the phrases of which they consist. Consider, for example:

	Categorial representation identical	*Functional representation different*
(13) Peter – killed – a millionaire	: NP–VP–NP	Su–P–DO
(14) Peter – died – a millionaire	: NP–VP–NP	Su–P–SA
(15) The porter – called – Jim – a taxi	: NP–VP–NP–NP	Su–P–BO–DO
(16) The porter – called – Jim – a fool	: NP–VP–NP–NP	Su–P–DO–OA
(17) Henry – married – Erica – in Paris	: NP–VP–NP–Prep.P	Su–P–DO–A
(18) Henry – reminded – Erica – of Paris	: NP–VP–NP–Prep.P	Su–P–DO–PC

	Functional representation identical	*Categorial representation different*
(19) Eric – writes – beautifully	: Su–P–A	NP–VP–Adv.P
(20) Eric – writes – every week	: Su–P–A	NP–VP–NP
(21) Eric – writes – in bed	: Su–P–A	NP–VP–Prep.P
(22) Fred – became – a doctor	: Su–P–SA	NP–VP–NP
(23) Fred – became – rich	: Su–P–SA	NP–VP–Adj.P

The examples above show that sentences are best described in functional and categorial terms at the same time. Such a description specifies not only the category of the constituents of which the sentence is composed, it also shows what function these constituents have. Sentence (8), for example, can be represented as in Figure 7.2, where the labelling refers to both functions and categories. Constituents appear inside the boxes, function-labels are printed over the boxes and category labels underneath.

Additional examples (not in the form of a tree-diagram):

(11)a. My boss – has bought – his daughter – a flat
      [Su: NP]   [P: VP]   [BO: NP]   [DO: NP]

(12)a. We – met – the Joneses – unexpectedly – in New York – last year
      [Su: NP] [P: VP]   [DO: NP]   [A: Adv.P]   [A: Prep.P.]   [A: NP]

With the exception of the function predicator, which is invariably realized by a verb phrase, sentence functions can be realized in a variety of ways.

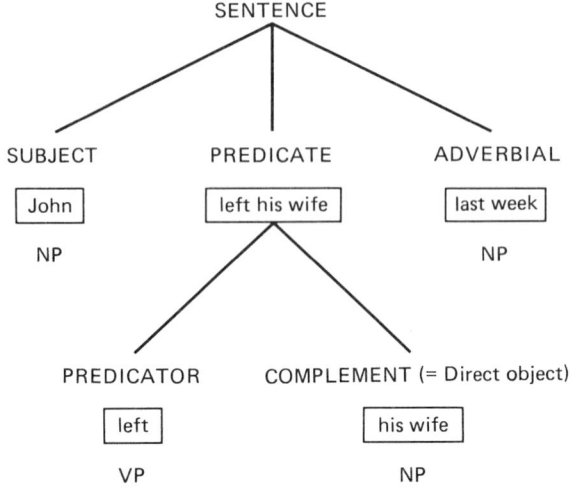

Figure 7.2

Thus the functions subject and direct object can be realized by noun phrases, as in sentences (1–23) above, but also, for example, by finite and non-finite clauses, as in:

(24) *That the men are unwilling to compromise* is obvious
(25) I regret *being unable to come tonight*

We shall not go any further into the relations between functions and their possible realizations at this stage. They are dealt with in detail in Chapter 8.

Sentence functions: syntactic and semantic criteria

Criteria for the identification of the functions mentioned above will be discussed in sections 7.2–7.4.

Sentence functions can be dealt with in semantic as well as in syntactic terms. We shall chiefly concentrate on syntactic criteria, but it may be useful to say something about the possibility of defining functions from a semantic point of view. For instance, if we consider

(26) *John* whipped the horse
(27) The police shot *the rioters*
(28) The burglar smashed the window *with a stone*

we might say that the italicized parts realize different functions, because they have different semantic roles, viz those of agent (26), victim (27) and instrument (28). One of the difficulties involved in defining sentence functions semantically is that there seems to be no one-to-one correspondence between semantic role and syntactic function. For example, in

(29) *The bomb* killed twenty spectators
(30) *Twenty spectators* were killed
(31) *The IRA* killed two secret agents

the italicized parts realize the function subject, if we apply the criteria of section 7.2. From a semantic point of view, all three are different; the subject in (29) is instrument, in (30) it is victim and in (31) agent.

The syntactic criteria that we shall apply in our discussion of sentence functions are of two kinds: they are based on observable as well as non-observable features. Among the observable features are position in the sentence and concord. Thus, in

(32) *Her husband* is a sailor
(33) *Their husbands* are sailors

the italicized constituents may be said to function as subject because of their position in the sentence (immediately before the verb phrase) and because of their concord relations (singular in (32): *is a sailor*; plural in (33): *are sailors*). Non-observable features are features that are not immediately apparent, but can be made visible by performing certain tests upon a sentence. Among the non-observable features are substitutability, passivizability and obligatoriness. To take substitutability first, in

(34) I gave *Mary* a present
(35) I bought *Mary* a present

one of the reasons why the constituent *Mary* in (34) may be said to have the function indirect object (see subsection 7.3.2.2) is the fact that a prepositional phrase introduced by *to* may be substituted for it, as in

(34)a. I gave a present *to Mary*

In (35) *Mary* has the function benefactive object (see subsection 7.3.2.3), since it can be replaced by a prepositional phrase introduced by *for*, as in

(35)a. I bought a present *for Mary*

The second non-observable feature, passivizability, can be made visible by testing whether a verb phrase is capable of occurring in the passive. If it is, the constituent following such a verb phrase is said to have the function direct object (see subsection 7.3.2.1). Consider, for example:

(36) John killed *Bill*
(37) He shook *the bottle*

where *Bill* and *the bottle* have the function direct object, because the passivization test shows that the verb phrases of the two sentences are passivizable, that is, can occur in acceptable sentences of the type: *X was killed by Y* and *X was shaken by Y*. Now, if we compare (36) and (37) with

(38) John killed *himself*
(39) He shook *his fist*

we find that there are passive sentences corresponding to (36) and (37), while there are no passive analogues to (38) and (39). Thus, we can have

(36)a. Bill was killed by John

but not

(38)a. *Himself was killed by John

In spite of the fact that passive counterparts to (38) and (39) are lacking, we say that *himself* and *his fist* function as direct object, since they are preceded by verb phrases that are passivizable. It should be borne in mind, therefore, that the passivization test is applied, not to a sentence as a whole, but only to the verb phrase. A condition here is that, under passivization, the verb retains its original meaning. This means that, in a sentence like

(40) I fail *to see your point*

the italicized constituent is not a direct object, for, although we have

(41) The test was failed by the majority of the students

the meaning of *fail* in (40) is different from the meaning of *fail* in (41).

There are cases where the verb phrase is followed by two complements, as in

(42) John gave Mary a watch
(43) John bought Mary a watch
(44) John called Mary a fool
(45) John compared Mary with his mother

where we have:

(42) indirect object + direct object (see subsection 7.3.2.2)
(43) benefactive object + direct object (see subsection 7.3.2.3)
(44) direct object + object attribute (see subsection 7.3.2.5)
(45) direct object + predicator complement (see subsection 7.3.2.6)

For sentences containing only one complement we use the passivization test to establish whether the complement is a direct object or not (cf 36–41). If the verb phrase is followed by two complements, the passivization test is of course not sufficient to differentiate between them, but must be supplemented by other tests.

Obligatoriness is the third of the non-observable features mentioned above. The term refers to the fact that certain constituents must be present; to leave them out would make the sentence unacceptable or change the meaning of the remaining constituents. For example, in

(46) You called Tom unco-operative last night

the constituents *you, called, Tom* and *unco-operative* are all obligatory, as can be seen from

(46) a. *—— called Tom unco-operative last night
      b. *You —— Tom unco-operative last night
      c. *You called —— unco-operative last night
      d.   You called Tom —— last night

where (a–c) are unacceptable and (d), although acceptable, has a different meaning from (46). In (46) there is one non-obligatory (or optional) constituent, viz *last night*, which may be left out without affecting either the acceptability of the sentence or the meaning of the other constituents:

(46)e. You called Tom unco-operative

One final observation should be made in connection with (46a). Although we have asterisked this sentence, there may be contextual conditions under which it is possible for the subject to be ellipted. This is the case, for instance, in

(47) You were angry with Peter and (you) called Tom unco-operative last night

Here we have two sentences with identical subjects, linked by coordination and that is why ellipsis of the subject of the second sentence does not affect its acceptability. For additional examples of ellipsis see subsection 4.3.2.2.

7.2 Subject

The function **subject** may be attributed to a constituent of a sentence on the basis of the following criteria:

1. Position
2. Concord
3. Passivization
4. Repetition in tag-questions

Position

In terms of position the function subject is associated with an obligatory constituent of the sentence which

(a) Precedes the verb phrase in

    1. Statements (both positive and negative)

(48) Last night *the Joneses* wanted us to babysit
(49) *Her father* has given her a tape-recorder
(50) *I've* never seen anything like it
(51) In that case *he* shouldn't have done it

    2. Questions, if this constituent is or contains one of the following items: *who, whose, what, which* and their compounds in *-ever*. Note that if the parts of the verb phrase are separated by a noun phrase, it is this noun phrase, and not the WH-item which is the subject (see b.3):

(52) *Who* knows this?
(53) *What* causes malaria?
(54) *Which* came first?

(55) Jim can't do this, but *whoever* can?
(56) *Who* can put up Henry tonight?
(57) *What* can be done about it?
(58) *Whose house* will be pulled down next?
(59) *Who* has never seen a hippopotamus?
(60) *Which subject* has not been discussed so far?

(b) Follows the (first word of the) verb phrase in

    1. Yes/no questions:

(61) Does *he* realize he is wrong?
(62) Was *last night's flight to New York* cancelled?
(63) Should *this word* be printed in italics?
(64) Are *they* in favour of America's foreign policy?
(65) Have *you* any idea where he went?
(66) I understand you want to go, but must *you*?
(67) Has *he* a car?

    2. Questions introduced by *when*, *where*, *why*, *how* and their compounds in *-ever*:

(68) When did *you* see the accused last?
(69) Where did *Harry* spend the night?
(70) Why is *the Government* so eager to enter the Common Market?
(71) How ever did *your little son* manage to get up there?

    3. Questions introduced by *who(m)*, *whose*, *what*, *which* and their compounds in *-ever*, if the verb phrase consists of more than one word:

(72) Who can *one* hold responsible?
(73) What have *they* been telling her?
(74) Which brand do *you* prefer?
(71) Who(m) do *the police* suspect?
(76) What can *the boys* have been doing last night?
(77) Whichever Smith do *you* mean?
(78) Whose car did *he* borrow?

Concord

In terms of concord the function subject is associated with that constituent which accounts for the presence of a sibilant suffix in the verb phrase, as in

(79) *John* hates his brothers
(80) *Mary* has written several interesting essays

Note that if the second noun phrase is singular, as in

(81) *John* hates his brother
(82) *Mary* has written an interesting essay

the function subject can only be identified by using other criteria.

The absence of a sibilant suffix in the verb phrases of the following sentences justifies the assignment of the function subject to the plural constituents:

(83) *Boys* love adventure
(84) *The girls* have done a good job

Again it should be noted that, if there are two plural noun phrases in a sentence, the concord criterion cannot be used. It goes without saying that the concord criterion is also irrelevant in cases where the finite verb does not formally distinguish between singular and plural, for instance with past tense forms and the present tense forms of modal auxiliaries.

Passivization

Thirdly, in active sentences the function subject can be attributed to that constituent which occurs in the *by*-phrase of the corresponding passive sentences:

(85) *The Pope* excommunicated the Cardinal →
     The Cardinal was excommunicated by *the Pope*
(86) *The policemen* threw the gangster into the river →
     The gangster was thrown into the river by *the policemen*

The *by*-phrase in question denotes the agent of the action. Local and temporal *by*-phrases in passive sentences are obviously irrelevant to this criterion. Compare:

(87) The man must have been stabbed *by the roadside*
(88) The decision will be announced *by noon*

Repetition in tag-questions

Finally, the function subject may be assigned to that constituent which is repeated in so-called tag-questions; in this type of question noun phrases are pronominalized:

(89) *John* hates girls, doesn't *he*?
(90) *It* is ten miles to your place, isn't *it*?
(91) *There* is no danger, is *there*?
(92) *Sheila* used to tutor John, didn't *she*?
(93) *These books* are not too expensive, are *they*?

Sometimes the identification of the function subject may present considerable difficulties. Ideally, all the criteria mentioned should be simultaneously applicable. This is by no means always the case. There are sentences for which most of the above criteria are not valid, for example those exhibiting inversion:

(94) In came *Jack*
(95) Behind them lay *the camp of the Indians*

(96) So soundly did *he* sleep that the bang did not wake him up
(97) Never had *I* seen him so embarrassed
(98) Rarely does *the man in the street* understand what politics is about

7.3 Predicate

The constituent functioning as subject is one of the two obligatory parts of the sentence. The second part of the sentence that is obligatory receives the function label **predicate**. In the examples below the obligatory parts appear in labelled brackets, the optional part(s) being unbracketed:

(99) [Birds] [sing] at dawn
     Su   Pred

(100) [The salt] [dissolved] quickly
      Su   Pred

(101) After a fortnight [the money] [had vanished] mysteriously
                        Su   Pred

(102) [Mr Smith] [was chairman] two years ago
      Su   Pred

(103) [The nightwatchman] [hit the burglar] with his torch
      Su   Pred

7.3.1 Predicator

From examples (99–103) it is clear that the part of the sentence realizing the function predicate may or may not be further segmentable into IC's. If it consists of a verb phrase only, the functions predicate and **predicator** are realized by the same constituent:

(104) Lions *roar*
(105) At dawn the party *set out*
(106) The jewels *had vanished*
(107) The man *was dying*
(108) Two of the prisoners *may have escaped*
(109) The child *should have been sleeping*
(110) The case *must have been being investigated* at the time

7.3.2 Complement

If the part of the sentence realizing the function predicate can be segmented, the functions of its IC's are predicator and complement (see Figure 7.2). The function **complement** is therefore associated with those elements of the predicate constituent that do not belong to the verb phrase. The presence or absence of a complement is determined by the lexical verb in the verb phrase (see subsection 2.2.4).

Examples (99–101) and (104–109) contain verbs that need not be followed by complements. The verbs in the following sentences, however, require one or more complements:

(111) Susan's parents gave *her a bicycle* on her birthday
(112) They are building *a new motorway* near Brixham
(113) The team is investigating *animal behaviour*
(114) Which doctor is treating *you*?
(115) Why does your wife use *Dr Spock's book*?
(116) The Prime Minister's position seems *desperate*
(117) Such things can make *life very difficult*
(118) The Chairman referred to *the proceedings of the previous meeting*
(119) We are still looking for *a solution*
(120) I suppose *that Jim is right*
(121) Do you think *that he will marry her*?
(122) Let's hope *that Jack will make it*
(123) Professors tend *to be conservative in their politics*
(124) After long discussions he condescended *to approve of the plan*

As appears from Figure 7.2, the function complement in the sentence *John left his wife last week* is realized by the noun phrase *his wife*. However, examples (111) and (117) show that there may be more than one complement in the same sentence, since in (111) *her* and *a bicycle* and in (117) *life* and *very difficult* are obviously constituents with different functions.

Complement types

We distinguish six complement types, for which we employ the following function labels:

1. direct object   (DO)
2. indirect object   (IO)
3. benefactive object   (BO)
4. subject attribute   (SA)
5. object attribute   (OA)
6. predicator complement (PC)

In general it can be said that in sentences containing complement verbs complements are obligatory constituents of the predicate constituent. However, the indirect object constituent is often omissible, as appears from sentences like

(125) The Johnsons sent (us) flowers
(126) Mary gave (him) a bottle of whisky

and the benefactive object constituent is omissible as well:

(127) Call (me) a porter, will you?
(128) Father is going to buy (himself) a Mini

We look upon the bracketed elements in sentences (125) and (126) as complements rather than adverbials (cf section 7.4) for two reasons:

1. their position in the sentence, unlike the position of the adverbial, is fixed, viz before the direct object constituent:
2. unlike the adverbial they can become the subject of a passive sentence. This property they share with the direct object.

The arguments for calling the bracketed constituents in sentences (127) and (128) complements rather than adverbials are that they have a fixed position in the sentence and that they are felt to be semantically related to indirect objects.

Complements can be divided into two classes: **single complements** and **companion complements**. Single complements are those that can occur independently in an English sentence. They are the direct object and the subject attribute. Companion complements cannot occur independently, but must be accompanied by a direct object. They are the indirect object, the benefactive object and the object attribute. Note that the predicator complement is either a single complement or a companion complement:

> single complement   : He takes *after his father*
> companion complement : You cannot compare John *with Mary*

In general all six complement types have fixed positions in the sentence (cf subsections 7.3.2.1–7.3.2.6). Most complement types may, however, be shifted to sentence-initial position for the sake of emphasis:

> direct object   : *This book* I do not understand
> subject attribute   : *Rich* he certainly wasn't
> object attribute   : *A liar* they have called him ever since
> predicator complement : *His father* he doesn't resemble

7.3.2.1 Direct object

A single complement may generally be said to function as **direct object** if it follows immediately after a verb phrase which (a) can occur in a passive sentence and (b) after passivization preserves its meaning (see the discussion of the passivization criterion in section 7.1). As the last three examples show, the lexical verb may also be a prepositional verb, a phrasal verb or a phrasal-prepositional verb:

(129) a. Shakespeare wrote *Hamlet*
      b. *Hamlet* was written by Shakespeare
(130) a. The Senate has discussed *this issue*
      b. *This issue* has been discussed by the Senate
(131) a. The police are investigating *this case*
      b. *This case* is being investigated by the police
(132) a. Our neighbours are looking after *the children*
      b. *The children* are being looked after by our neighbours

(133) a. All students should look up *these words*
      b. *These words* should be looked up by all students
(134) a. The treasurer will check up on *these figures*
      b. *These figures* will be checked up on by the treasurer

If the verb phrase is followed by two complements both of which can become the subject of a passive sentence, then the first of these is the indirect object (see subsection 7.3.2.2), the second the direct object.

If conditions (a) and (b) above are not met, the obligatory constituent following the verb phrase is a predicator complement (see subsection 7.3.2.6).

7.3.2.2 Indirect object

The function **indirect object** is associated with the first of two complements, both of which are characterized by their ability to function as subject in a corresponding passive sentence:

(135) a. The local Council has awarded *him* a scholarship
      b. *He* has been awarded a scholarship by the local Council
(136) a. The University granted *Professor Harvey* leave of absence
      b. *Professor Harvey* was granted leave of absence by the University
(137) a. Next year Mr Juarez will teach *us* Spanish
      b. Next year *we* shall be taught Spanish by Mr Juarez
(138) a. His father gave *him* a good talking-to
      b. *He* was given a good talking-to by his father

Another characteristic of the indirect object constituent is its substitutability by a *to*-phrase following the direct object constituent. Compare:

(139) a. The firm offered *Jim* the job
      b. The firm offered the job *to Jim*
(140) a. Why did your brother show *his fiancée* the letter?
      b. Why did your brother show the letter *to his fiancée*?
(141) a. We have given *the personnel officer* your application
      b. We have given your application *to the personnel officer*

However, with a small group of verbs the indirect object constituent cannot be replaced by a *to*-phrase:

(142) Suddenly the centre-forward struck *the referee* a heavy blow
(143) The judge fined *him* £5
(144) I don't think he can forgive *her* her rudeness
(145) Your suggestion will save *the company* a great deal of money
(146) Do you really envy *him* his expensive car?
(147) You can spare *yourself* the trouble
(148) That shop in Bond Street charged *me* £10 for that tie

7.3.2.3 Benefactive object

As far as its position in the sentence is concerned, the constituent functioning as *benefactive object* resembles the indirect object; it immediately precedes the direct object constituent. It can also be substituted for by a prepositional phrase, which usually requires the preposition *for*, not *to*, as in the case of the indirect object:

(149) After his retirement he bought *his daughter* a villa in the country
(150) Could you call *me* a taxi?
(151) Fetch *me* a paper, will you, Jack?
(152) Mary is bound to cook *you* a very good dinner tonight
(153) She made *herself* a cup of tea
(154) Why did he refuse to play *us* the Moonlight Sonata?
(155) My father wrote *me* my French essay

Another criterion distinguishing the benefactive object from the indirect object is that the former cannot, as a rule, become the subject of a passive sentence:

(156) **I* was fetched my hat
(157) **I* was written my French essay

7.3.2.4 Subject attribute

The function **subject attribute** is associated with a constituent which complements the verb and is related to the subject of the sentence. This relationship is such that what is expressed by the subject attribute constituent is predicated of the subject. This can be done directly, as in (158), where we have a copula verb linking the subject and the subject attribute. The relationship can also be expressed without an explicit verb, as in (172), which may be paraphrased as: 'Her husband was a Catholic when he died'. The subject attribute constituent usually follows the verb phrase.

(158) Your boss is *a nice fellow*
(159) When did he become *Archbishop of Canterbury*?
(160) That prophecy won't come *true*
(161) Very few jobs have fallen *vacant* lately
(162) I feel *rotten* today
(163) She always gets *too emotional*
(164) Let's go; it's growing *dark*
(165) Throughout the trial he kept *quiet*
(166) This looks *pretty suspicious*
(167) At the end of the demonstration the mob ran *riot*
(168) The prisoner's case seems *hopeless*
(169) Mrs Johnson's hair has turned *grey* overnight
(170) The first day of my weekend in Brighton turned out *wet*
(171) That criterion doesn't hold *good* in all cases
(172) Her husband died *a Catholic*

(173) Our team emerged *easy victors* in last year's competition
(174) After all his experiences in Australia he returned *a wiser man*

Note that some of the verbs in the above examples may also be followed by a direct object, as in (175–179). In that case their meaning is evidently different:

(175) The doctor felt *my pulse*
(176) He's growing *a beard*
(177) Derek has kept *a diary* ever since he was 10
(178) Your wife makes *delicious cakes*
(179) Can you prove *this*?

7.3.2.5 Object attribute

We have already considered sentence-patterns of the type:

(180) He gave Charles a monkey

where the verb phrase is followed by two noun phrases, functioning as indirect object and direct object respectively. A superficially similar pattern is found in

(181) He called Charles a monkey

In (181), however, the constituent *a monkey* does not function as direct object, since it cannot become the subject of the passive equivalent of this sentence. If *a monkey* is not the direct object constituent, the other noun phrase, *Charles*, cannot be the indirect object constituent (cf subsection 7.3.2.2). From the fact that *Charles* can become the subject of the passive counterpart of (181) we may conclude that it is this constituent which functions as the direct object. Here, then, we have a sentence-pattern where the verb phrase is followed by two noun phrases, the first of which functions as direct object, the second having a function which we will call **object attribute**. Between the direct object constituent and the object attribute constituent there is a relationship such that what is expressed by the object attribute is predicated of the direct object constituent. In some cases it is possible to bring out this relationship by means of a paraphrase sentence containing a copula verb. Cf:

(182) a. Everybody considers your neighbour a fool
       b. Everybody considers your neighbour to be a fool

Other examples are:

(183) The witness called the accused *a murderer*
(184) Chelsea appointed him *manager*
(185) When did the club make this *a condition for membership?*

The function object attribute may also be realized by an adjective phrase:

(186) I find this solution *quite unacceptable*

(187) The next experiment proved the professor *wrong*
(188) Would you call the plan *unworkable?*
(189) Some idiot has painted my front door *blue*

All of the above examples can be passivized. For instance:

(184) a. He was appointed *manager* by Chelsea
(189) a. My front door has been painted *blue* by some idiot

It is obvious that object attributes in active sentences (like *manager* and *blue* in (184) and (189)) become subject attributes in the corresponding passive sentences.

7.3.2.6 Predicator complement

Strictly speaking, the term **predicator complement** could be used with reference to all those constituents that obligatorily complement the verb. However, we shall here use it in a restricted sense to denote an obligatory constituent which does not meet the criteria we have used to define the other five complement types. Thus, in (190-193), the italicized constituents function as predicator complements, not as direct objects, since they are preceded by verbs that cannot be passivized (eg *cost* and *resemble*) or, if they can, do not preserve their meaning (eg *contain* and *take*):

(190) His house in Hampstead must have cost *thousands of pounds*
(191) The boy resembles *his father*
(192) That tin contains *tobacco*
(193) The introduction of the metric system has taken *a lot of time*

As appears from the above examples, the predicator complement can be realized by a noun phrase. In addition it has the following realizations: a prepositional phrase (194), a finite clause (195), and a non-finite clause (196):

(194) During the party thieves stole *into the house*
(195) I bet *that he won't return the book in time*
(196) After a few minutes it began *to rain*

If the predicator complement is realized by a non-finite clause containing a *to*-infinitive, the infinitive may be preceded by a noun-phrase functioning as direct object of the finite verb, as in:

(197) Mother persuaded Mary *to see a doctor*
(198) He forced me *to empty my pockets*
(199) Why don't you encourage Walter *to emigrate?*
(200) Could you help me *to move this cupboard?*

We interpret (197) as follows:

Mother persuaded Mary [Mary to see a doctor]

that is, we look upon *Mary* as the direct object of *persuade*, while recognizing at the same time a subject-predicate relation between *Mary* and *see*. With respect to the analysis of (197) the question now arises whether we should call *Mary* the direct object of *persuade* or the subject of *see*. We prefer the former analysis in view of the fact that it is impossible to interpret the whole construction *Mary to see a doctor* as having the function direct object of *persuade*. On the other hand, a comparison of (197) and

(201) Mother would like Mary to see a doctor

shows that the latter requires a different analysis. Here we cannot interpret *Mary* as the direct object of *like*, so that we analyse as follows:

Mother would like [Mary to see a doctor]

The bracketed portion functions as direct object, realized by a non-finite clause with an explicit subject. The difference between (197) and (201) appears from the fact that the former has an alternative construction with a finite clause, whereas the latter has not:

(197) a. Mother persuaded Mary that she should see a doctor
(201) a. *Mother would like Mary that she should see a doctor

Another difference between sentences (197) and (201) is that the noun phrase preceding the non-finite clause can become the subject of a passive sentence in the former, but not in the latter:

(197) b.   Mary was persuaded to see a doctor
(201) b. *Mary would be liked to see a doctor

7.4. Adverbial

As appears from Figure 7.1 (see p. 127) the function **adverbial** is associated with a constituent which, in the tree-diagram, occupies a position on the same level as the subject and predicate constituents. In other words, like the subject and predicate constituents, the adverbial is treated as an IC of the sentence. In section 7.3 we have already pointed out that sentences consist of two obligatory IC's, viz the subject constituent and the predicate constituent. It follows that the adverbial is a non-obligatory constituent of the sentence. Consider:

(202) Dick and Susan are getting married *next week*
(203) I have not paid my subscription *since last year*
(204) The bartender killed his best friend *in a fight*
(205) John is washing his car *in the garage*
(206) *Even in this form* the plan is unacceptable
(207) David *often* drinks port
(208) *Desperately* he tried to wrench open the lock
(209) *For the sake of clarity* we will give two more examples
(210) Derek *quietly* left the room
(211) *Probably* he is in London

Adverbials are characterized by two properties:

1. their optionality: they can be left out without any resultant changes in the meaning of the remaining part of the sentence;
2. their mobility: they can often occupy more than one position in the sentence. For instance, the adverbials in the last two examples could occur in sentence-initial, sentence-medial and sentence-final position. Compare:

    (a) *Quietly* Derek left the room
    (b) Derek *quietly* left the room
    (c) Derek left the room *quietly*

    (a) *Probably* he is in London
    (b) He is *probably* in London
    (c) He is in London, *probably*

7.5 Summary

By way of conclusion all the sentence functions discussed in the present chapter are set out in Table 7.1.

Table 7.1

SENTENCE	Subject: Su (obligatory)			
	Predicate (obligatory)	Predicator: P		
		Complement	single	Subject Attribute : SA Direct Object : DO Predicator Complement : PC
			companion	Indirect Object : IO Benefactive Object : BO Object Attribute : OA Predicator Complement : PC
	Adverbial: A (optional)			

The rules for English sentence structure yield the following basic patterns:

1. Subject-Predicator-(Adverbial)   : Su P (A)
2. Subject-Predicator-Subject Attribute-(Adverbial) : Su P SA (A)
3. Subject-Predicator-Direct Object-(Adverbial)   : Su P DO (A)
4. Subject-Predicator-Predicator Complement-(Adverbial)   : Su P PC (A)
5. Subject-Predicator-Indirect Object-Direct Object-(Adverbial)   : Su P IO DO (A)
6. Subject-Predicator-Benefactive Object-Direct Object (Adverbial)   : Su P BO DO (A)
7. Subject-Predicator-Direct Object-Object Attribute-(Adverbial)   : Su P DO OA (A)

8. Subject-Predicator-Direct Object-Predicator
   Complement-(Adverbial)   : Su P DO PC (A)

Examples:

1. Lions roar
2. Your boss is a nice fellow
3. Shakespeare wrote *Hamlet*
4. The boy resembles his father
5. Mary lent her boyfriend five pounds
6. She made herself a cup of tea
7. He called Charles a monkey
8. You cannot compare John with Mary

8. The structure of the sentence: Realizations

8.1 Introductory

As we have already observed in Chapter 7, the same category may realize different functions and the same function may be realized by different categories. What makes the relation between **function** and **realization** so complicated is the almost complete absence in English of a one-to-one correspondence between them. Describing this relation would be easy, if it were the case that a particular function could only be realized by a particular realization type. In fact, such a one-to-one correspondence exists only between the function predicator and the verb phrase. Realization types are our main concern in this chapter, that is for each function we shall exemplify the various ways in which it can be realized. Before we do so, it is necessary to discuss briefly the notion of multiple realization of functions.

Multiple realization

In our discussion of the various ways in which sentence functions are realized (section 8.2 ff) we only illustrate cases of **single realization**, that is realization of a sentence function by means of one phrase or clause. Note, however, that all sentence functions allow **multiple realization**, that is realization by means of two or more coordinated phrases or clauses. Some examples are:

Su: (1) *John and Mary* are a very nice couple
P: (2) We *buy and sell* used cars
SA: (3) The problem is *that John is lazy and Mary very energetic*
DO: (4) Phil teaches *French and English*
OA: (5) I consider that plan *impossible, unrealistic and absurd*
A: (6) You will have to do it *carefully and with a great deal of tact*

We also speak of multiple realization in the case of appositions where two noun phrases do not only realize the same function, but also have identical reference. Note that the second member in an apposition may be an emphatic *-self* pronoun. This pronoun may be moved to the end of the sentence if it is part of the realization of the subject:

(7) *The Dorchester, one of London's most expensive hotels,* has been bought by Arabs
(8) *The former chairman of our club, Fred Harrington,* is now a millionaire
(9) *John himself* did it (= *John* did it *himself*)

8.2 Subject

The function subject can be realized by:

1. a noun phrase
2. a finite clause
3. a non-finite clause
4. anticipatory *it* + finite/non-finite clause
5. unstressed *there* in existential sentences
6. a prepositional phrase

Noun phrase

Noun phrases range in complexity from simple items like nouns and pronouns (10–15), to more complex structures (16–19):

(10) Has *Lucy* dyed her hair?
(11) *Blood* is thicker than water
(12) *Something* is wrong, I'm sure
(13) *Who* rang you up last night?
(14) *It*'s now been raining for six days
(15) *It* suddenly fell off the table

(16) *All these new bungalows* were bought by foreigners
(17) *The last three houses on the right-hand side of the street* are going to be pulled down
(18) *The girl you were talking to* is my secretary
(19) *The book that John wrote about the political situation in Zambia* is selling well

Finite clause

Two types of finite clause can realize the function subject: *that*-clauses and clauses containing an initial *WH*-item:

(20) *That he is the best candidate* is self-evident
(21) *That Michael has not contributed to this volume* is odd
(22) *That the President is now prepared to negotiate* is regarded as a hopeful sign
(23) *That his wife has left him* does not make him unhappy
(24) *That she rings you up every night* must be a bit of a nuisance

(25) *What is said in chapter six* is irrelevant
(26) *Whether he will be able to come* is an open question
(27) *Which of them is going* will be decided tomorrow
(28) *Where the new plant will be built* is up to the government
(29) *Why the news was not released earlier* will be explained tomorrow
(30) *How the gang managed to open the safe* is a mystery
(31) *When we leave* does not matter

Non-finite clause

Two types of non-finite clause can realize the function subject: those containing an infinitive with *to* (32–36) and those containing an *-ing* participle (37–42). Note that if the infinitive clause has a subject of its own, it must be introduced by *for* (32). Infinitive clauses can be introduced by *WH*-words (34–36).

(32) *For John to marry a girl like Alice* would mean the end of his career
(33) *To make such a statement in public* is a bit of a risk
(34) *How to classify these items* was a problem for the librarian
(35) *Whether to finance this scheme or not* is a question to be answered later
(36) *What to do in the case of emergency* is fully explained in the leaflet

(37) *Howard being away* does not bother me
(38) *A woman being appointed to such a high post* is still exceptional today
(39) *Getting here* took a day and a half
(40) *Opening the doors* has virtually no effect on the temperature
(41) *Having the exact fare ready* makes the bus go faster
(42) *Saying that you are sorry* won't help you

Anticipatory it + finite/non-finite clause

Sentences like:

(20) a. That he is the best candidate is self-evident
(33) a. To make such a statement in public is a bit of a risk

have the following alternative constructions:

(20) b. It is self-evident that he is the best candidate
(33) b. It is a bit of a risk to make such a statement in public

In (20a) and (33a) the function subject is realized by a finite and non-finite clause respectively. The difference between the (a) and the (b) sentences is that in the (b) examples the clauses occur in sentence-final position, which necessitates the use of *it* at the beginning of these sentences. We therefore say that in (b)-type sentences the function subject is realized by the discontinuous constituent *it* + finite/non-finite clause (a discontinuous constituent is one whose IC's do not follow each other immediately). The first IC of this constituent may be said to anticipate the second. For this reason it is traditionally called **anticipatory** *it*. It should be noted that not all sentences containing anticipatory *it* have (a)-type alternatives. Thus, corresponding to (44) there is no (44a):

(44)   It would seem that he has been wrong all the time
(44) a. *That he has been wrong all the time would seem

Sentences with anticipatory *it* exhibit a wide range of patterns. We shall distinguish six main types:

(a) *it* + predicator (active) + clause
(b) *it* + predicator (passive) + clause

(c) *it* + predicator (active) + subject attribute + clause
(d) *it* + predicator (passive) + subject attribute + clause
(e) *it* + predicator + direct object + clause
(f) *it* + predicator + direct object + object attribute + clause

(a) It + *predicator (active)* + *clause*

In this pattern the verb is always intransitive, the clause either finite (43–47) or, rarely, non-finite (48–50):

(43) From this *it* follows *that the experiment was successful*
(44) *It* would seem *that he has been wrong all the time*
(45) *It* does not matter *what he thinks of us*
(46) *It* looks *as though a visit to the zoo is out*
(47) *It* does not sound *as if your prestige needed raising*

(48) *It* does not matter *destroying the food*
(49) *It* wouldn't do *to tell Peter now*
(50) When sailing in light winds, *it* pays *to move about very gently*

(b) It + *predicator (passive)* + *clause*

In this pattern the predicator is passive and the clause either finite (51–56) or non-finite (57–59):

(51) *It* has been suggested *that these two phenomena are related*
(52) *It* is now claimed *that such guarantees were never given*
(53) *It* must be doubted *whether he will come*
(54) *It* was pointed out *how frequently this had happened*
(55) *It* is not known *if this film will be released in Holland*
(56) *It* might be asked *why this policy failed*

(57) *It* is hoped *to get the students to vote Labour*
(58) *It* is planned *to publish the anthology in March*
(59) At last night's meeting *it* was agreed *to ban all overtime*

(c) It + *predicator (active)* + *subject attribute* + *clause*

In this pattern the verb is intransitive (usually *be*). The subject attribute may be realized by a noun phrase, an adjective phrase or a prepositional phrase. In each case the clause may be either finite or non-finite.

Subject attribute realized by noun phrase:

(60) *It* is time *you were beginning to think of your future*
(61) *It* is not the case *that he has lost all his money*
(62) *It* is not a matter of indifference *whether you come or not*
(63) *It* is a pity *that Jack has changed his mind*
(64) *It* is such a bore *when people do things they don't have to*

(65) *It* would be much more sense *for me to do it at once*
(66) *It* is the most natural thing in the world *for boys to be after girls*

(67) *It* is not his business *to interfere*
(68) *It* will be our principal purpose *to seek to reduce east-west tension*
(69) *It* was a pleasure *meeting you*
(70) *It* is no use *tackling this problem now*
(71) *It* is a drag *having to make new friends again*

Subject attribute realized by adjective phrase:

(72) *It* seems unlikely *that they will join us*
(73) *It* is clear *that Arsenal will not stand much of a chance*
(74) *It* remains problematic *whether he will come*
(75) *It* is astonishing *how much she has enjoyed her outings*
(76) *It* is not irrelevant *where the conference will be held*
(77) *It* is far too long *since you were my guest*

(78) *It* may be necessary *for the protein level in some animal foodstuffs to be reduced*
(79) *It* would have been more accurate *to have said so*
(80) *It* has proved possible *to identify the body*
(81) How lovely *it* is *to see you again*!
(82) *It* was difficult *getting lifts on the M1*
(83) *It* is silly *talking about unity when we do not put it into practice*
(84) Do you think *it* is odd *having guests for the weekend*?

Subject attribute realized by prepositional phrase:

(85) *It* is of importance *that we should book in advance*
(86) *It* is to the credit of the present régime *that it publicized these scandals*
(87) *It* is not in line with your promise *that you have turned up tonight*
(88) *It* is in the nature of plans *to go wrong*
(89) *It* is just like him *to say a thing like that*
(90) *It* was out of the question *dealing with him in a reasonable way*

(d) It + *predicator (passive) + subject attribute + clause*

In this pattern the subject attribute is realized by a noun phrase or an adjective phrase. The clause may again be finite or non-finite.

Subject attribute realized by noun phrase:

(91) *It* was considered a mistake *that the Ambassador had left his post*
(92) *It* has been interpreted as a sign of weakness *that we make concessions so willingly*
(93) *It* was thought an honour *to have such a distinguished scholar on the staff*

Subject attribute realized by adjective phrase:

(94) *It* was considered odd *that the meeting was adjourned*
(95) *It* was regarded as indecent *for girls to wear bikinis*
(96) *It* was deemed impossible *to terminate the negotiations before the deadline*

(e) It + *predicator* + *direct object* + *clause*

The clause in this pattern may be finite or non-finite:

(97) *It* surprised me *that the Johnsons were in time*
(98) *It* struck the policeman *that the car had a foreign number-plate*
(99) *It* shocked the Board *to hear the chairman announce his resignation*
(100) *It* offended Paul *to be told that he was not wanted*

(f) It + *predicator* + *direct object* + *object attribute* + *clause*

In this pattern the object attribute is realized by a noun phrase, an adjective phrase or a prepositional phrase. The clause is either finite or non-finite:

(101) *It* made him the unhappiest man in the world *when his wife left him*
(102) *It* drove the headmaster mad *that the boys were so lazy*
(103) *It* keeps Dad in good condition *that he runs two miles every morning*
(104) *It* made Louise happy *to see her son prosperous*
(105) *It* would drive me round the bend *to have to go to an office every day*

Unstressed *there*

Unstressed *there* functions as subject in so-called **existential sentences**, that is, in sentences of the type

(106) *There* is a book on the table
(107) *There* was a pause
(108) *There* was no reply
(109) *There* have been problems in the past
(110) Has *there* been any reason for suspicion?
(111) *There* is no invitation for us, is *there*?

in which *there* is followed by a form of *be* plus a noun phrase. This phrase, which is usually indefinite, we call the **notional subject** of the sentence.

We consider *there* to be the subject in existential sentences, although of the four criteria that we have mentioned in connection with the identification of the function subject (cf section 7.2) it meets only two, viz position and repetition in tag-questions. The concord criterion is somewhat problematic. Normally the form of *be* is determined by the number of the following noun phrase:

(112) *There* is a student who wants to see him
(113) *There* are three students who want to see him

This would argue in favour of calling the noun phrase following *be* the subject. In colloquial English, however, we come across sentences like

(114) *There*'s three students who want to see him
(115) I think *there*'s a good few people think that Labour will win

(116) The problem is rather more complicated when *there*'s so many variables

so that the concord criterion had perhaps better be ignored.

The best argument for calling *there* the subject in sentences like (112) and (113) is the fact that it is repeatable in tag-questions. Compare:

(112) a. *There* is a student who wants to see him, isn't *there*?
(113) a. *There* are three students who want to see him, aren't *there*?

Unstressed *there* also occurs in active sentences containing verbs other than *be* (117–124), as well as in passive sentences (125–130):

(117) *There* stood an enormous statue in the hall
(118) *There* does not appear to have been any change in their views
(119) *There* seems little doubt that he is right
(120) This showed that *there* also took place a chain decomposition
(121) *There* remains a discrepancy between the two interpretations
(122) Close to each funnel *there* develops a tangle of blood-vessels
(123) Through the door *there* came the faint creak of the rocking-horse
(124) *There* comes a point when the reason in mathematics begins to fail

(125) In 1929 *there* was committed the most serious crime in the history of the United States
(126) It seems to me *there* may be a few lessons learned by many seaside resorts
(127) I suppose that *there* is local food brought in and sold in the locality
(128) As *there* are about 200 expected to go, we shall be busy, I suppose
(129) *There*'s also included in this class a lot of other things
(130) *There* aren't many murderers executed in this country

Prepositional phrase

The function subject may be realized by a prepositional phrase, which, as the examples show, usually denotes either time or place:

(131) *After five o'clock* is the best time to meet
(132) *Throughout the afternoon* would be too long
(133) *By the roadside* is not an ideal place for a picnic
(134) *Within two miles of the airport* would be too noisy

In many sentences of the type exemplified above the subject can also be realized by adverbial pro-forms like *now*, *then*, *here* and *there*. Cf:

(131) a. *Now* is the best time to meet
(134) a. *Here* would be too noisy

8.3 Predicate

As was pointed out in section 7.3, the constituent realizing the predicate function is one of the two obligatory parts of the sentence. If this constituent does not allow segmentation (in other words, if it consists of a verb phrase only) we have sentences in which one constituent realizes the functions predicate and predicator at the same time, as in:

(135) Dogs bark
(136) He laughed

If segmentation is possible, two functions can be distinguished: predicator and complement. For their realization see subsections 8.3.1 and 8.3.2.

8.3.1 *Predicator*

As the examples in subsection 7.3.1 illustrate, the predicator is a constituent that is usually realized by verbal forms only. Exceptions are:

1. Phrasal verbs (sequences of verb + adverb):

(137) He *looked up* the number
(138) Their supplies *were running out*

2. Prepositional verbs (sequences of verb + preposition):

(139) He *was looking for* his wallet
(140) Why *did* you *send for* the doctor?

3. Phrasal-prepositional verbs (sequences of verb + adverb + preposition):

(141) I *get on with* him perfectly
(142) My sister *goes in for* pop-music

4. Verb + noun + preposition idioms:

(143) The terrorists *set fire to* the police-station
(144) Newspapers *keep track of* current events
(145) We *lost touch with* him

Note that there are sequences of verbal forms which do not qualify as realizations of the predicator function, but should be analysed as predicates in which the predicator is followed by a predicator complement:

(146) Peter wants to leave
(147) He appears to be in control
(148) I don't want to be forced to get to know him better

8.3.2 *Complement*

Any immediate constituent of the predicate that is not part of the predicator has the function complement. We have already seen that six complement types can be distinguished:

1. direct object
2. indirect object
3. benefactive object

4. subject attribute
5. object attribute
6. predicator complement

In subsection 7.3.2 examples have been given of verbs that may be followed by more than one complement. Note that complement types 2, 3 and 5 generally presuppose the presence of type 1, and that types 1, 2, 3, 5 and 6 are mutually exclusive with 4:

(149) He gave *his son a watch* (2 + 1)
(150) He bought *his son a bike* (3 + 1)
(151) He called *his son a liar* (1 + 5)

8.3.2.1 Direct object

The function direct object can be realized by:

1. a noun phrase
2. a finite clause
3. a non-finite clause
4. anticipatory *it* + finite/non-finite clause

Noun phrase

There is no difference between the structure of noun phrases realizing the function subject and that of noun phrases realizing the function direct object. Both functions can be realized by simple as well as by complex noun phrases, although the latter tend to occur more frequently as realizations of the function direct object than as realizations of the function subject.

(152) I suddenly recognized *the postman*
(153) *Who(m)* has John been ringing up?
(154) The driver of the ambulance couldn't see *anything*
(155) At last they are publishing *Professor Smith's course in linguistics that he gave at Harvard two years ago*
(156) They have now finished *the twenty-storey hotel near the supermarket on the corner of Painswick Road*

Finite clause

There are two types of finite clause that can realize the function direct object: *that*-clauses and *WH*-clauses. They occur in sentences containing passivizable verb phrases.

That-clauses may require anticipatory *it* in the passive construction. Compare the following sets of examples:

(157) a. They now deny that a mistake has been made
       b. That a mistake has been made is now denied
       c. It is now denied that a mistake has been made

(158) a.   They say that the President committed suicide
       b.   *That the President committed suicide is said
       c.   It is said that the President committed suicide

We say that the *that*-clauses in (157a) and (158a) are both realizations of the function direct object. In each case the clause follows a verb phrase which can occur in a passive sentence without change of meaning (see section 7.1), as appears from sentences (157b), (157c) and (158c). That *deny*, unlike *say*, allows two passive constructions is irrelevant to our argument.

Additional examples of *that* -clauses functioning as direct object are:

(159) John admitted *that he was wrong*
(160) We hope *that the expedition will be a success*
(161) We agreed *that we would meet at six o'clock*
(162) I think *that this would be extremely unwise*
(163) You should not forget *that he is over 80 now*
(164) Farmers in Wales claimed *that they had seen flying saucers*
(165) Father suggests *that she go at once*
(166) We all regretted *that his departure should have been so sudden*

Like *that*-clauses, *WH*-clauses are considered to realize the function direct object if they are preceded by a passivizable verb phrase. Hence the *WH*-clause in (167a) is not a direct object clause because of the ungrammaticality of (167b) and (167c):

(167) a.   We wonder where he is
       b.   *Where he is is wondered
       c.   *It is wondered where he is

The verb phrase preceding the *WH*-clauses in (168a) and (169a), on the other hand, may occur in passive sentences, as appears from (168b), (168c) and (169b). That *reveal*, unlike *affect*, allows two passive constructions is irrelevant to our argument:

(168) a.   Last night they revealed who had done it
       b.   Who had done it was revealed last night
       c.   It was revealed last night who had done it
(169) a.   This crisis will affect whatever chances of a settlement there are
       b.   Whatever chances of a settlement there are will be affected by this crisis
       c.   *It will be affected by this crisis whatever chances of a settlement there are

Additional examples of *WH*-clauses functioning as direct object are:

(170) They do not know *what our long-term prospects are*
(171) Why don't you listen to *what he is saying*?
(172) Scotland Yard have discovered *where the gang are hiding*
(173) Tomorrow we shall discuss *when the next meeting is to take place*

(174) Psycholinguists are investigating *how language is acquired*
(175) We shall never find out *why Kennedy was assassinated*
(176) Labour are now building *whatever suits their housing policy*
(177) The Department will organize *what the Faculty is asking for*
(178) I do not know *whether he is in*

Non-finite clause

Three types of non-finite clause can function as direct object, viz infinitive clauses, *-ing* clauses and *-ed* participle clauses. An infinitive clause may or may not contain the particle *to*. If it does not, the clause must have an explicit subject (179–184). If the infinitive is preceded by *to*, the subject of the clause may be explicit (185–192) or implied (193–201). In the latter case the infinitive may be preceded by a *WH*-word (198–201). The subject of a *to*-infinitive may occasionally be preceded by *for* (192). Non-finite *-ing* clauses may or may not have an explicit subject (202–208 and 209–213, respectively). An *-ed* participle clause always has an explicit subject (214–217).

At first sight it would seem that in sentences containing non-finite clauses with an explicit subject the subject noun phrase of the clause might be said to function as the direct object of the preceding finite verb phrase, especially since, in a number of cases, we have passive counterparts, as in

(179) a. Bob was seen to crash into a lamppost
(184) a. Jim has never been known to do such irresponsible things

However, such an analysis is counter-intuitive on semantic grounds. For example, in (179) the speaker does not claim that he saw Bob, but that he saw the event of Bob crashing into a lamppost. Similarly, in (184) what the speaker claims is not that he has never known Jim, but that, in his experience, Jim has never acted irresponsibly. Hence our analysis of sentences like (179) and (184) is:

(179) I saw [Bob crash into a lamppost]
(184) I have never known [Jim do such irresponsible things]

Examples:

(179) I saw *Bob crash into a lamppost*
(180) Did anyone hear *Jerry come home last night?*
(181) Sue felt *the sweat trickle down her spine*
(182) We shall have to make *him resign*
(183) They let *him go*
(184) I have never known *Jim do such irresponsible things*
(185) I would like *Peter to give me a ring at 8*
(186) Dad would certainly prefer *you not to go there on your own*
(187) Jack would hate *his daughter to marry a Welshman*
(188) We have always known *him to be a hard worker*
(189) Let's assume *this to be a feasible proposition*

(190) The jury believed *the youth to be guilty of arson*
(191) I understand *this to have been a mistake*
(192) I will arrange *for father to sign the documents*

(193) The TUC decided *to continue the strike*
(194) The lovers arranged *to meet in a pub*
(195) Hooligans attempted *to break into the cricket pavilion*
(196) The Board desired *to have the blueprint available at an early stage*
(197) We'll try *to leave before dawn*

(198) We did not know *what to do*
(199) They have never learned *how to apply these rules*
(200) They could not decide *where to go*
(201) The organizing committee are considering *who to invite*

(202) We could not stop *him getting into mischief*
(203) Your father cannot prevent *them getting married*
(204) Please, excuse *John barging in like this*
(205) I watched *Mary crossing the street*
(206) The old woman must have heard *the burglar coming upstairs*
(207) She felt *his hand trembling on her shoulder*
(208) I remember *Freddy saying that*

(209) Most people enjoy *having breakfast in bed*
(210) More and more men under thirty are giving up *smoking*
(211) Most children prefer *cycling* to walking
(212) Many novelists have tried *writing short stories*
(213) Clare had to cancel *coming to dinner*

(214) My daughter saw *the old lady beaten up*
(215) In the narrow alley we found *ourselves surrounded by a street gang*
(216) I've never heard *Mozart sung in French*
(217) I felt *my curiosity roused by this news*

Anticipatory it + finite/non-finite clause

Just as *it* + finite/non-finite clause realizes the function subject in

(20) b. *It* is self-evident *that he is the best candidate*
(33) b. *It* is a bit of a risk *to make such a statement in public*

so *it* + finite/non-finite clause realizes the function direct object in sentences of the type

(218) I resented *it that John was late*
(219) They considered *it* impossible *to get there in time*

Additional examples of anticipatory *it* + finite clause:

(220) We took *it* for granted *that Jack would be there*
(221) The public consider *it* improper *that he is still in office*
(222) We cannot get *it* across to him *that this is difficult*
(223) They would regard *it* as a mistake *if you left*

Additional examples of anticipatory *it* + non-finite clause:

(224) I think *it* unlikely *for my son to do a thing like that*
(225) I would look upon *it* as a blunder *for Ian to write that letter*
(226) I leave *it* to you *to finish this*
(227) The committee found *it* very hard *to settle the issue*
(228) You must find *it* exciting *being so much in the limelight*

8.3.2.2 Indirect object

The function indirect object is normally realized by a noun phrase and only very rarely by a finite *WH*-clause:

(229) The IRA sent *the British Ambassador* a letter-bomb on his birthday
(230) The parish accorded *the new vicar* a warm welcome
(231) He showed *his friends* his stamp collection
(232) The security-guards gave *whoever entered the bank* a penetrating look

8.3.2.3 Benefactive object

Like the indirect object the benefactive object is normally realized by a noun phrase and, rarely, by a finite *WH*-clause:

(233) Shall I pick *you* an apple?
(234) We'll get *Jimmy* a new pair of shoes tomorrow
(235) My father bought *whoever came in* a beer

8.3.2.4 Subject attribute

The function subject attribute can be realized by:

1. a noun phrase
2. an adjective phrase
3. a prepositional phrase
4. a finite clause
5. a non-finite clause

Noun phrase

(236) Martin will make *a good husband*
(237) The President's death will forever remain *a mystery*
(238) Acapulco is *the best place there is to spend a holiday*
(239) Your proposal seems *a good solution*
(240) They parted *good friends*
(241) His son came home *a decrepit wreck*

In the following sentences the subject attribute is realized by a noun phrase which functions as the object attribute in the corresponding active sentences (see subsection 8.3.2.5). Note that after certain verbs the noun phrase is introduced by *as*:

(242) Newton was elected *President of the Royal Society*
(243) Who was appointed *manager of the new branch*?
(244) The young prince was crowned *king* by the Archbishop
(245) The victim was identified *as the son of the mayor*
(246) This behaviour might be described *as a symptom of mental illness*

Adjective phrase

(247) Then, suddenly, everything went *black*
(248) He appeared *glad to see me*
(249) His theory proved *entirely wrong*
(250) The threat of another nuclear catastrophe looms *large* in this part of the world
(251) The sandstorm continued *unabated* for 48 hours
(252) Your coffee smells *good*
(253) That proposal sounds *quite interesting*

Like noun phrases, adjective phrases can function as subject attribute in passive sentences. After certain verbs the adjective phrase is introduced by *as*:

(254) Mrs Bonnington was found *guilty* by the jury
(255) The window was pushed *open*
(256) This scheme was regarded *as impracticable*

Prepositional phrase

(257) My eldest brother is *in the United States*
(258) Mary feels *on top of the world*
(259) The party was *on Wednesday*
(260) John's conduct was *above all praise*
(261) When we arrived, half the boat was *under water*

Finite clause

(262) His theory is *that mutations are not brought about by chance*
(263) The question is *whether there is enough to go round*
(264) Andrew does not want to be *what his father was*
(265) Things remained *as they had been in the past*
(266) That was *when he had gone away to London*
(267) That firm was made *what it is today* by Sir Keith Hamilton

Non-finite clause

Two types of non-finite clause can realize the function subject attribute: infinitive clauses and *-ing* clauses. The infinitive is usually preceded by *to*, in which case the non-finite clause may be introduced by a *WH*-word. It must be introduced by *for* if the infinitive has an explicit subject. Clauses containing *-ing* may or may not have an explicit subject.

(268) The Government's first concern will be *to strengthen the economy*
(269) The problem is *where to hide it*
(270) The question is *whether to invite him or not*
(271) The difficulty is *who to appoint next*
(272) The thing to do is *for us to take the appropriate measures*
(273) All you have to do is *(to) ask for further information*
(274) What I do is *go out and buy a sandwich*
(275) Visiting Athens is *seeing Greece at its best*
(276) The most surprising thing was *John being elected chairman*
(277) That may be called *putting the cart before the horse*

8.3.2.5 Object attribute

The function object attribute can be realized by:

1. a noun phrase
2. an adjective phrase
3. a prepositional phrase
4. a finite clause
5. a non-finite clause (rare)

Noun phrase

(278) He named his new yacht *Marina*
(279) When did they elect Newton *President of the Royal Society*?
(280) Whom did they appoint *manager of the new branch*?
(281) *What* do they call their son?
(282) I consider John *the only man that can do this job properly*
(283) We are convinced that his presence would make the congress *a success*
(284) Freddy and Joan christened their baby *Christopher*
(285) The Archbishop crowned the young prince *king*

After certain verbs the object attribute is introduced by *as* (the verb *take* may be followed by both *as* and *for*, the verb *mistake* only by *for*):

(286) All the critics regard his latest novel *as the best he has ever written*
(287) The police identified the victim *as the son of the mayor*
(288) Would psychiatrists describe this behaviour *as a symptom of mental illness*?
(289) Do you take me *for a fool*?
(290) When I said this, she took it *as an insult*
(291) Sorry, I mistook you *for my wife*

Adjective phrase

(292) Such incidents tend to make things *very difficult*
(293) The jury found Mrs Bonnington *guilty*
(294) Do you prefer your whisky *neat*?
(295) He rubbed the windscreen *dry*
(296) He pushed the window *open*
(297) I regard this scheme *as impracticable*

Prepositional phrase

(298) Put your head *on my shoulder*
(299) Jim keeps his Jaguar *in perfect order*
(300) Clifford left the room *in a mess*
(301) We do not count Edgar *among our friends*
(302) Laura imagined her husband *in her sister's arms*
(303) We found the headmaster *in a good mood*
(304) She wears her hair *in a coil*

Finite clause

(305) At last the University appointed him *what he had always wanted to be*
(306) Sir Keith Hamilton made the firm *what it is today*
(307) Why don't we call this structure *what all other grammarians call it*?
(308) Paint the door *whatever colour you like*

Non-finite clause

(309) I call that *putting the cart before the horse*
(310) He regarded this *as being the worst mistake I ever made*
(311) She interpreted the passage *as having been written specially to insult her*

8.3.2.6 Predicator complement

The function predicator complement can be realized by:

1. a noun phrase
2. a prepositional phrase
3. a finite clause
4. a non-finite clause

Noun phrase

(312) That suit doesn't fit *me*
(313) He has *two houses in the country*
(314) Does this box contain *sugar*?
(315) Does Mary's husband really weigh *15 stone*?

(316) His plans lack *wisdom*
(317) The expression on his face meant *trouble*
(318) My study measures *six metres* across
(319) Four times two equals *eight*
(320) This new plane seats *400 passengers*
(321) The journey will take *two hours*
(322) He is always acting *the fool*
(323) That remark must have escaped *him*

Prepositional phrase

(324) Suddenly a rabbit darted *across the tennis-court*
(325) She quickly slipped *into her dressing-gown*
(326) His family belonged *to the aristocracy*
(327) When the headmaster came in, Tom slunk *from the room*
(328) This has never occurred *to me*
(329) On the Continent all traffic must keep *to the right*
(330) This reminds me *of my schooldays*
(331) They charged the colonel *with murder*
(332) You cannot compare this dictionary *with Roget's Thesaurus*
(333) At last we convinced him *of his mistake*
(334) John combines intelligence *with humour*
(335) This book provides the student of English *with a thorough coverage of the basic facts of English syntax*
(336) The book plunged literary America *into a heated controversy*

There is a superficial similarity between sentences (330–336) and (298–304), since in both cases the finite verb is followed by a noun phrase and a prepositional phrase. Compare:

	VP	NP	Prep. P
(304) She	wears	her hair	in a coil
(330) This	reminds	me	of my schooldays

In both sentences the noun phrase functions as direct object. However, the prepositional phrases are not functionally equivalent. In (304) the prepositional phrase functions as object attribute because of the subject-predicate relation between *her hair* and *in a coil* (cf: *her hair is in a coil*; see subsection 7.3.2.5). In (330) there is no such relation (cf: **I am of my schooldays*) and therefore the only function that the prepositional phrase can have is that of predicator complement.

Finite clause

(337) Ray used to brag *that every actress fell in love with him*
(338) Teachers complain *that classes are getting too big*
(339) This means *that we shall have to check our data again*
(340) Do you mind *if I smoke?*

(341) He grumbled *that things were no longer what they used to be*
(342) I marvel *why Martha should want to marry an academic*
(343) This device will ensure *that the engine starts smoothly*
(344) We wonder *where he is*
(345) Doris convinced the policeman *that he was wrong*
(346) The Electricity Board should have warned the public *that power cuts might occur*
(347) This reminds me *that I have not paid my subscription yet*

Non-finite clause

All types of non-finite clause can realize the function predicator complement: infinitive clauses, *-ing* clauses and *-ed* participle clauses. Some infinitive clauses in this function require the particle *to* and do not have an explicit subject (348–366). Examples (357–366) illustrate a type of infinitive clause preceded by a direct object which is also the implicit subject of the non-finite clause (see the analysis of sentence (197) in subsection 7.3.2.6). *-Ing* clauses may or may not occur with an explicit subject (367–370 and 371–377, respectively). *-Ed* participle clauses, which are rare in this function, have an explicit subject (378–380).

(348) The policeman affected *not to hear me*
(349) The Vice Chancellor condescended *to listen to the protests of the students*
(350) In James's later novels his style tends *to become more and more involved*
(351) He failed *to see what was the matter with her*
(352) When John took his degree, I happened *to be in London*
(353) Does the company stand *to lose anything by this transaction*?
(354) How did you get *to know him*?
(355) We have come *to understand his problems better*
(356) Would you care *to come round for a drink*?

(357) They forced their prisoner *to make a full confession*
(358) Why does not she advise him *to give up*?
(359) We would ask you *to reconsider your decision*
(360) The unions told their members *not to put in any overtime*
(361) Why do not you persuade him *to start next year*?
(362) We must urge you *to send in your application at once*
(363) The sergeant ordered his men *to line up*
(364) She begged him *not to marry the girl*
(365) I'll trust you *to do it*
(366) The doctor encouraged Wilson *to go on a diet*

(367) Would you mind *John opening the window*?
(368) This news will no doubt start *him thinking*
(369) I cannot stand *him making such silly remarks*
(370) Fancy *Peter doing a thing like that*!
(371) He didn't bother *getting any tea*

(372) How long will she go on *insulting him*?
(373) It kept *raining for hours*
(374) When I hear him lecture, I can't help *laughing*
(375) The Government's proposals will mean *working overtime*
(376) Next year this firm will cease *manufacturing hearing-aids*
(377) When he said this, the audience burst out *laughing*

(378) The chairman could not make *himself heard*
(379) In the match against Arsenal Peters had *his leg broken*
(380) You should get *your hair cut*

8.4 Adverbial

The function adverbial can be realized by:

1. an adverb phrase
2. a prepositional phrase
3. a noun phrase
4. a finite clause
5. a non-finite clause
6. a verbless clause

Adverb phrase

(381) The explosion occurred *suddenly*
(382) Why did you arrive *so late*?
(383) *Slowly* they pushed the car up the hill
(384) Peter and Jane seem to get on *very well*
(385) We have now been waiting *long enough*
(386) The children are playing *outside*
(387) We have a meeting *now and then*
(388) I left my luggage *over there*
(389) He ran *as fast as he could*
(390) They pulled *so energetically that the rope broke*
(391) The baby now walks *much better than we had expected*
(392) He is ill. *Consequently* he can't come
(393) *Quite surprisingly*, he passed the exam

Prepositional phrase

(394) John was washing his car *in the garage*
(395) *At the end of Chippendale Avenue* we turned right
(396) *After two hours* the party arrived
(397) Elvis Presley used to be very popular *in the sixties*
(398) Army experts handled the bomb *with the utmost care*
(399) That boy is, *without any doubt*, the most promising student we have
(400) *In all frankness*, I don't believe a word of what you say
(401) *In this way* the Liberals will never achieve their purpose
(402) *On top of that* he asked me to come to his office

Note that the function adverbial can also be realized by a prepositional phrase in which the prepositional complement is an *-ing* clause (403–410), an *-ed* participle clause (411–414) or a verbless clause (415–418). If the clause has an explicit subject it is introduced by *with* or *without*. The *-ing* clause is the only clause type that may occur without an explicit subject:

(403) *With the term not being on*, it's a bit difficult getting a babysitter
(404) The guerillas got away *without a shot being fired at them*
(405) *With meat being so expensive*, we'd better buy lamb chops
(406) This part of the diary was published *without John being consulted*
(407) *By telling him about it* you might very well spoil everything
(408) *On arriving at the station* I found that the taxi-drivers were on strike
(409) *In making our analysis* we must take account of this factor
(410) *Apart from being incomplete* the book is historically unreliable

(411) *With the President murdered*, the country had become ungovernable
(412) He managed to persuade us, *with hardly a word said*
(413) The refugees were squatting in the yard, *with their blankets draped around them*
(414) *Without a new chairman elected*, we cannot hope to be able to organize next year's exhibition properly

(415) *With the car ready*, we can now set off
(416) *With John away from home*, the children are difficult to handle
(417) *Without Peter in the chair*, the meeting is bound to end before six
(418) *With arms akimbo*, the woman stood shouting at us from the balcony

Noun phrase

(419) Did you see the Ambassador *last week*?
(420) They must have heard us quarrel *next door*
(421) Why don't you look at it *the way we do*?
(422) I'm sure they've met *many times*
(423) I don't like her *a bit*
(424) His plane may arrive *any minute*
(425) *The moment he entered*, I told him the news

Finite clause

Finite clauses functioning as adverbial may be classified on semantic grounds as:

clauses of place	(426–427)
clauses of time	(428–430)
clauses of concession	(431–433)
clauses of condition	(434–436)
clauses of reason	(437–438)
clauses of result	(439–440)
clauses of purpose	(441–442)
clauses of comparison	(443–444)
clauses of manner	(445–446)
clauses of proportion	(447–448)

(426) You may go *wherever you like*
(427) The accident happened *where the two roads cross*
(428) *As he listened*, his face became pale
(429) He can't be appointed *until he's had a medical examination*
(430) We'll write *as soon as we arrive*

(431) *Although he's only guessing*, he's probably right
(432) *Even if his account is true*, the police are not likely to believe him
(433) *Whatever you say*, I'm not going to change my mind

(434) *If the team want to win next week*, they will have to do better than this
(435) I'll give you a call *in case I can't make it*
(436) We won't have a theatre, *unless we get financial support*

(437) He went home, *because he had promised his wife to be back in time*
(438) *Since I don't share his views*, I shall vote against

(439) The boy stood on a chair, *so that he could reach the top shelf*
(440) The taxi-driver drove fast, *so that we got to Euston in time*

(441) Put it on the table *so that we can look at it*
(442) These cars were returned to the factory *in order that their drive-shafts should be replaced*

(443) They behaved *as though the room belonged to them*
(444) You're talking *as if you knew all about it*

(445) We did it *as we had been taught*
(446) Dennis talks to his children *as I do to my students*

(447) *As he grew older*, he became more cynical
(448) The temperature decreases *as you approach the window*

Non-finite clause

All types of non-finite clause can function as adverbial: infinitive clauses, *-ing* clauses and *-ed* participle clauses. With a few exceptions they express the same range of meanings as finite clauses functioning as adverbial.

Infinitive clause

Infinitive clauses always contain *to*, except when introduced by *rather than* and *sooner than*:

(449) *Rather than study*, Sam watched the football game
(450) *Sooner than leave his post*, the Ambassador was prepared to be killed

Infinitive clauses are of two types. In those of the first type the infinitive has a subject of its own, which is preceded by *for*:

(451) The Joneses vacated the house *for the new tenants to move in*
(452) I'd have given anything *for John not to have failed that exam*
(453) *For this plan to be feasible* unemployment must be reduced

In infinitive clauses of the second type the subject of the infinitive is not overtly expressed, but is understood to be the same as the subject of the main clause. Note that in examples (457–459) the infinitive is preceded by subordinators.

(454) That morning James woke up *to find his wife gone*
(455) *To understand his lectures* one must have some knowledge of logic
(456) *To hear him talk*, you'd think he was the boss
(457) He shook his head *as if to signal his disapproval*
(458) I left my luggage at the station *so as not to keep you waiting*
(459) They walked on tiptoe *in order not to disturb anyone*

The following examples are exceptions to the rule which says that the 'understood' subject of the infinitive clause is identical with the subject of the main clause. The 'understood' subject may be said to be 'I' or 'we':

(460) *To speak frankly*, Jim is not the man we want
(461) His resignation came quite unexpectedly, *to tell you the truth*
(462) *To put it bluntly*, £1,000 is not enough
(463) John's English, *to say nothing about his French*, is impeccable
(464) *To begin with*, ours is a world that changes too quickly

-Ing clause

-Ing clauses are of two types. Those of the first type have an explicit subject:

(465) 'How delightful', cried Robin, *her face lighting up*
(466) They were talking to each other, *neither listening to what the other was saying*
(467) *The referee being ill*, the match had to be postponed
(468) *Jack being what he is*, it's no use trying to persuade him
(469) This autobiography consists of three parts, *each dealing with an episode in the author's life*
(470) *All houses in the street having been searched*, the police disappeared again
(471) *Parliament being in recess*, this question will not be discussed until the autumn session
(472) The victim was lying on his back, *blood trickling from his nose*
(473) Nicholas leant back, *his mouth trembling slightly*
(474) *Weather permitting*, we shall go to Oxford tomorrow
(475) Next year Granddad will celebrate his ninetieth birthday, *God willing*

-Ing clauses of type two have no explicit subject: the 'understood' subject is identical with the subject of the main clause. They may be introduced by a subordinator (486–489):

(476) *Being rather short of money*, we decided not to go abroad
(477) *Having lived in London for some time*, he ought to know his way about
(478) The chairman refused to consider our proposal, *saying that it had not been properly discussed*
(479) *Reading between the lines*, we can discover almost as much about the author as about his subject
(480) Professor Jones spoke in a very soft voice, *thus making it impossible for us to follow his lecture*

(481) Brian was easy with his money, *buying drinks right and left*
(482) *Passing through the hall*, the Prime Minister was greeted by loud cheers
(483) *Looking out of the window*, you couldn't see the mountains for the clouds
(484) *Having said this*, we must now qualify the point made above
(485) *Having been punished so often*, the child has become very stubborn

(486) *When speaking English*, Peter often makes mistakes
(487) *While sitting in the sauna*, Joe Vanelli had a heart-attack
(488) *Though feeling rather excited*, the girls tried not to show it
(489) He suddenly sat down *as if trying to demonstrate how tired he was*

As we have seen above, there are examples of infinitive clauses that are exceptions to the rule that the implied subject of the infinitive clause should be identical with the subject of the main clause. Similar exceptions are to be found in the case of *-ing* clauses. Again the 'understood' subject may be said to be 'I' or 'we':

(490) *Putting it mildly*, his contribution is uninteresting
(491) *Considering all this*, why should his resignation interfere with the party's future?
(492) *Generally speaking*, it doesn't rain much here
(493) *Granting this to be true*, what conclusions can be drawn?

-Ed participle clause

Like infinitive clauses and *-ing* clauses, *-ed* participle clauses fall into two types. In clauses of the first type the subject is explicit:

(494) *Given these facts*, how are we to interpret them?
(495) *Granted the importance of the Prime Minister's speech*, it does not follow that the party is committed to what he said
(496) *This problem once solved*, we will have no difficulty in finishing the project
(497) *The letters posted*, he got into his car and tore off
(498) He peered at the stone, *a monocle screwed into his eye*
(499) *Hands raised*, the prisoners walked by in single file
(500) *All his energy spent*, he now wished to retire at last
(501) *His clothes caught in the barbed wire*, he could not escape
(502) *The money once invested*, you cannot withdraw it
(503) *Our task completed*, we breathed a sigh of relief
(504) *This said*, it has to be conceded that the book falls short of our expectations

In *-ed* participle clauses of type two the subject is understood and is identical with the subject of the main clause. They may be introduced by a subordinator (514–521):

(505) The day drifted by, *spoiled by tiny events*
(506) *Fortified by a glass of brandy*, he felt a warm glow spread over him

(507) *Born in 1855*, he spent his early years in England
(508) *Encouraged by this success*, Conrad wrote another novel
(509) *Left a widow at the age of 30*, Mrs O'Rourke returned to Ireland
(510) *Judged as a work of art*, this painting is of inferior quality
(511) *Written after the failure of his political ambitions*, the book is an attempt at self-justification
(512) *Challenged by these discoveries*, our team decided to continue
(513) *Set in the desert country of New Mexico*, this novel tells the story of a man's search for the truth

(514) This kind of analysis, *when done properly*, can yield surprising results
(515) *Once published*, the book is bound to have a tremendous impact
(516) Household linen, *if required*, will be supplied
(517) *When looked at from a syntactic point of view*, this sentence is unacceptable
(518) *Though intended for family reading*, these memoirs have now been published
(519) A dog will turn away, *if looked steadily in the eye*
(520) He sank down in a chair, *as if stunned by the news*
(521) *Unless kept to a minimum*, footnotes will put the reader off

The *-ed* participle clauses in the following sentences have no explicit subject. In a sense, the subject is recoverable from the context, but it is very difficult to describe the nature of the relation between the non-finite clause and the rest of the sentence. Perhaps the 'subject' of the *-ed* participle clause may be said to be the rest of the sentence in examples (522) and (523), and to refer to what has just been said in examples (524) and (525):

(522) *Stated bluntly*, what you say is ludicrous
(523) *Unless otherwise stated*, all books are in good condition
(524) *Put in a nutshell*, he is mad
(525) *Put more strongly*, to say that he was there at the time is tantamount to saying that he is guilty

Verbless clause

Two types of verbless clause can be distinguished: those with an explicit subject (526–530) and those without (531–545). Clauses of the second type may open with a subordinator (541–545):

(526) *His hands deep in his pockets*, the man stood watching the fight
(527) *Her clothes in disorder*, Olga ran out of the flat
(528) The newcomer hesitated in the doorway, *his hat in his hand*
(529) *His eyes wide open*, the injured man lay on the pavement
(530) *His feet up on the table*, he talked at great length about his exploits in Africa

(531) *An Irishman*, he had always felt unhappy in England
(532) *A crack shot*, he was invited to join the expedition
(533) *One of the wealthiest men in the country*, Lord Vickers has donated £100,000 to the National Trust

(534) *A staunch supporter of Labour's policy*, he would never criticize the Government
(535) *An orphan at the age of six*, Tom was brought up by a distant relative
(536) *Unaware of the danger*, the children were playing on the upper deck
(537) *Stubborn as ever*, Jack refused to make the next move
(538) *Reluctant to give in*, he tried to brazen it out
(539) *Very angry at what had happened*, the teacher threw Jimmy out
(540) *However inelegant*, this solution seemed the only practicable one

(541) *Though very ill*, Mary went on teaching
(542) *When ready*, these TV sets will be shipped at once
(543) *Whether cheap or expensive*, the house is too big for us
(544) *If available at all*, these goods will be hard to get
(545) *Although not fully fit*, John decided to play

Note that in (531–535) the NP does not function as the subject of the verbless clause, but, like the adjective phrases in (536–540), functions as its subject attribute.

The implied subject of the verbless clause need not be identical with the subject of the main clause, but may be *it* or *there*:

(546) *If possible*, I'll meet you at the station
(547) We can always take a later boat, *if necessary*
(548) Complaints, *if any*, should be made to the management

Note also that in imperative sentences containing a verbless clause both the main clause and the verbless clause may have an implied *you* as subject:

(549) *If in doubt*, consult your GP

8.5 Summary

The various possibilities for the realization of the functions in English sentences are set out in Table 8.1.

Table 8.1

Function		Realization							
							Clause		
		NP	Prep. P	Adj. P	Adv. P	VP	Finite	Non-finite	Verbless
Subject		+(1)	+				+(2)	+(2)	
Predicate	Predicator					+(3)			
	Complement DO	+					+(4)	+(4)	
	IO	+					+(5)		
	BO	+					+(6)		
	SA	+	+	+			+	+(7)	
	OA	+	+	+	+		+(8)	+	
	PC	+	+				+	+	
Adverbial		+	+		+		+	+	+

(1) includes *there* in existential sentences
(2) includes cases with anticipatory *it*
(3) includes phrasal, prepositional and phrasal-prepositional verbs, as well as verb + noun + preposition idioms
(4) includes cases with anticipatory *it*
(5) *WH*-clauses only
(6) *WH*-clauses only
(7) infinitive and *-ing* clauses only
(8) *WH*-clauses only

Appendix: A guide to sentence analysis

In this guide some examples will be given of how sentences can be analysed (for a list of abbreviations see page 183). The analysis of a sentence may be thought of as a procedure involving a number of discrete steps. The final result of the analysis is a tree-diagram (to be read from left to right) in which every constituent has received a function-category label, that is a label which indicates what function the constituent has in a larger whole as well as to what category it belongs.

The number of steps involved in the procedure is determined by the number of structural levels in the sentence, that is by the number of times that function-category labels have to be assigned to constituents that together make up a larger constituent. To put this in terms of a tree-diagram, the number of steps depends on the number of (sets of) nodes intervening between the top node and the bottom nodes of the tree. This can be illustrated by means of the unlabelled tree-diagram below, which represents the structure of sentence

(1) *After the war in Europe many people in this country emigrated to America.*

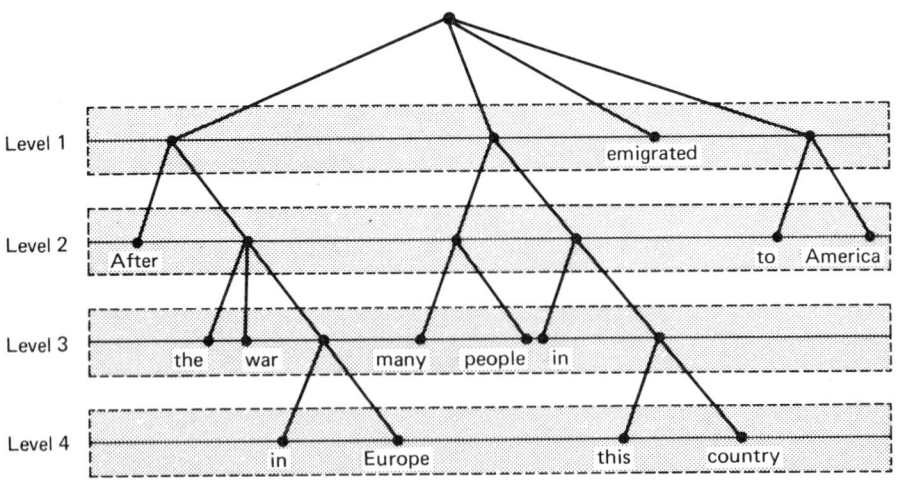

As the diagram shows, sentence (1) has four levels of structure. Whenever a particular level contains a constituent that is capable of further analysis, this analysis takes place on a lower level. For example, of the four constituents on level 1, three are capable of further analysis, which is carried out on level

2. This process is continued until the lowest level is reached, which contains constituents that cannot be segmented any further.

Since function-category labels have to be assigned to constituents at each level, the analysis of sentence (1) consists of four steps. Each step in the analysis consists of two sub-steps: one in which all constituents on a particular level receive a function label and one in which they are assigned to the appropriate categories. The order of the two sub-steps is irrelevant and can be reversed; in other words, category assignment may precede function identification.

The various steps involved in the analytical procedure are described in greater detail below in the analysis of sentence (2), which, like sentence (1), requires four steps:

(2) *Many students in this department can speak*
    two foreign languages fluently

Step 1

(a) On the basis of your interpretation of the sentence establish its immediate constituents and identify their function.

Sentence (2) consists of three functional constituents:

    Subject   : Many students in this department
    Predicate : can speak two foreign languages
    Adverbial: fluently

For the sake of brevity we shall henceforth skip the predicate in our analyses. This means that a sentence will be immediately segmented into Subject, Predicator, Complement(s) (if any) and Adverbial(s) (if any), rather than into its immediate constituents. Step 1 therefore also involves the identification of the Predicator and the Direct Object of sentence (2). The Predicator is *can speak* and the Direct Object is *two foreign languages*. It is now possible to say which sentence pattern sentence (2) belongs to: Su – P – DO – A.

(b) Identify the categories by which the functional constituents are realized.

In sentence (2) the Subject is realized by a noun phrase, the Predicator by a verb phrase, the Direct Object by a noun phrase and the Adverbial by an adverb phrase:

    Many students in this department :   Su   : NP
    can speak   :   P   : VP
    two foreign languages   :   DO : NP
    fluently   :   A   : Adv.P

Step 2

This step involves the description of the structure of the categorial constituents identified in step 1(b). It consists of two sub-steps:

(a) Establish the immediate constituents of the categorial constituents identified in step 1(b) and describe them in terms of their function.

For example, the subject noun phrase *Many students in this department* consists of three immediate constituents: *many* (which functions as determiner), *students* (which functions as head) and *in this department* (which functions as postmodifier).

(b) Describe the immediate constituents of the categorial constituents identified in step 1(b) in terms of the categories to which they belong.

Many is a quantifier, *students* is a noun and *in this department* is a prepositional phrase.

Steps 3 and 4

Step 3 (which involves the analysis of the prepositional phrase *in this department*) and step 4 (which involves the analysis of the noun phrase *this department*) follow the familiar function-category assignment routine.

The complete analysis of sentence (2) is as follows:

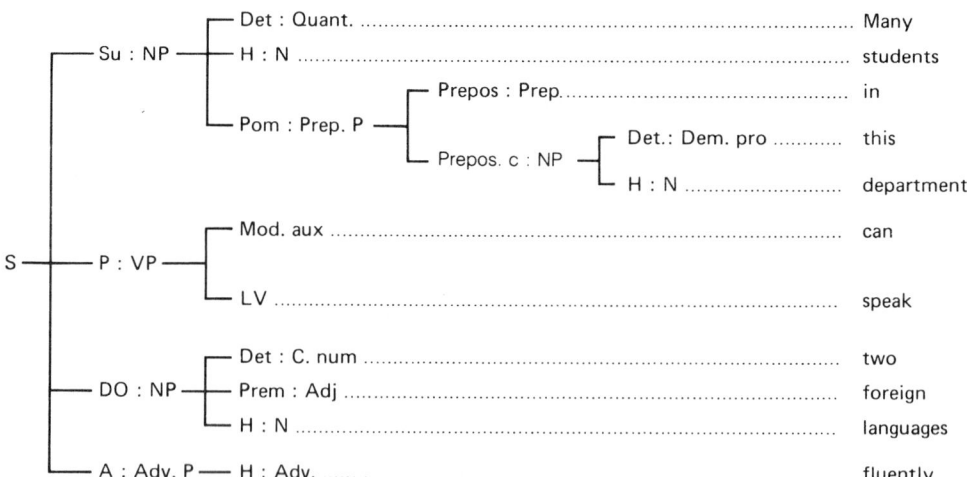

The above tree-diagram should be read from left to right as follows: this sentence (S) consists of a Subject (Su), a Predicator (P), a Direct Object (DO) and an Adverbial (A). The Subject **is realized by** (= a : b) a noun phrase, which **consists of** $(= a \overline{\overline{\overline{}}}\!\begin{smallmatrix} x \\ y \\ z \end{smallmatrix})$ a determiner, a head and a postmodifier, realized by a quantifier, a noun and a prepositional phrase respectively, etc.

The procedure sketched above applies only once to simple sentences like (2). As was observed above, however, the number of steps involved depends on the structural complexity of the sentence to be analysed. For example, if a sentence contains one or more clauses, the procedure has to be repeated for every clause. Consider, for instance, sentence

(3) *John believes that he will be appointed if he applies when he is 21*

The relationship between the whole sentence (a) and the various clauses (b), (c) and (d) can be represented as follows:

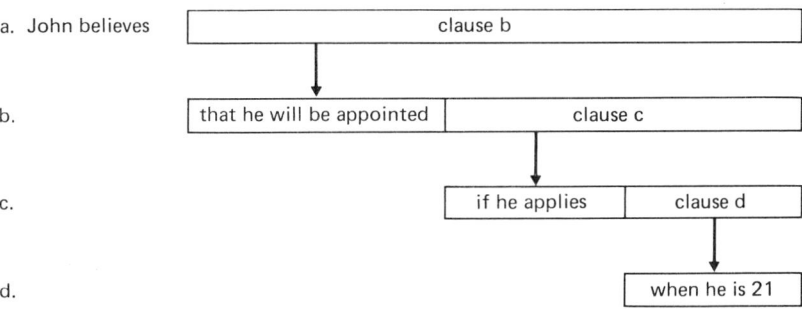

The analytic procedure first applies to (a) and subsequently to each of the clauses (b), (c) and (d). The analyses are as follows:

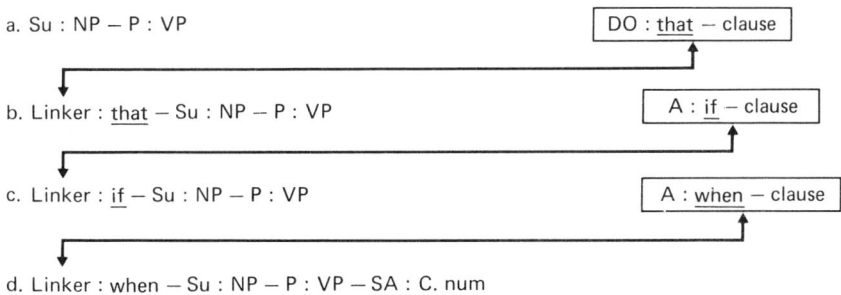

In other words, (d) functions as Adverbial in (c), which functions as Adverbial in (b), which functions as Direct Object in (a).

The complete analysis of sentence

(3) *John believes that he will be appointed if he applies when he is 21*

is as follows:

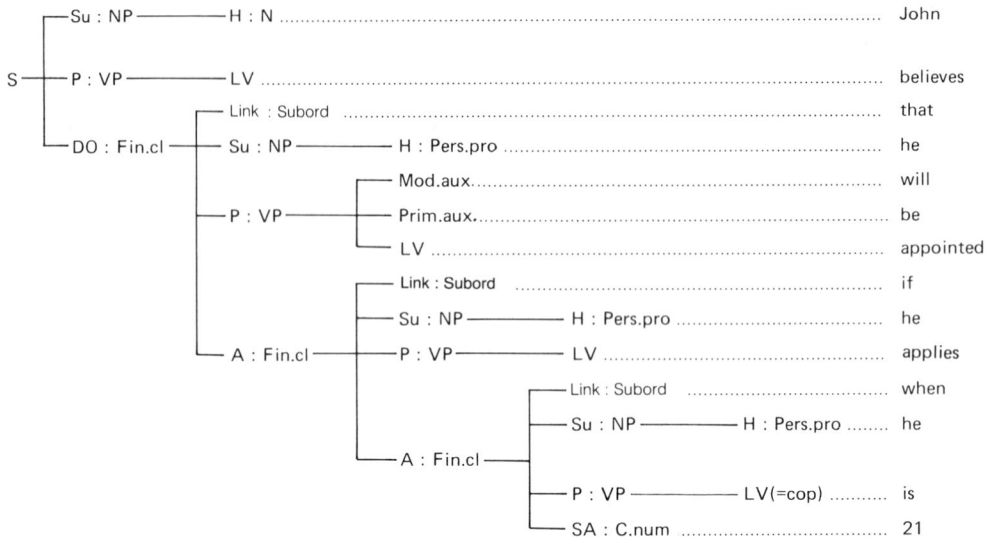

Sentence (3) is a complex sentence, since the function DO is realized by a (finite) clause. Sentence pattern: Su–P–DO.

The following are additional examples of the analysis of simple sentences. Note that elements of discontinuous constituents appear in triangles and are linked by broken lines.

(4) *The men talked at great length about their exploits in Africa*

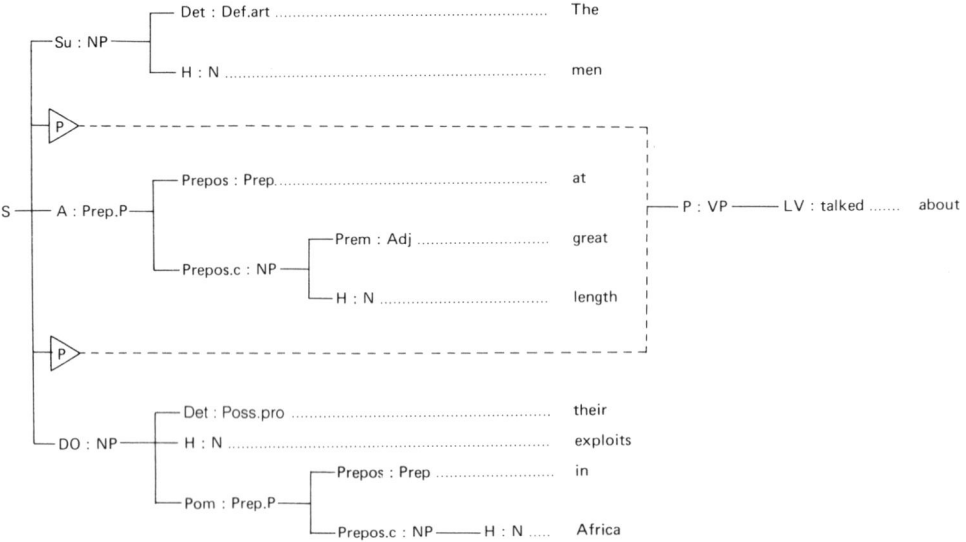

Sentence (4) is a simple sentence.
Sentence pattern: Su—▷P▷—A—◁P◁—DO

(5) *Jim has always been very proud of the success that his children had at school*

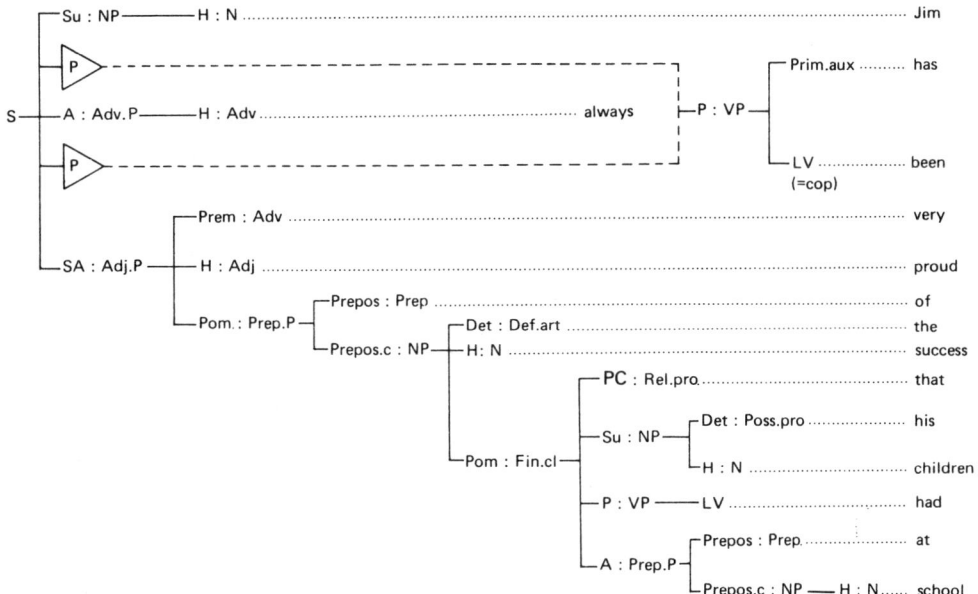

Sentence (5) is a simple sentence.

Sentence pattern: Su—P—A—P—SA

(6) *A better solution had been found than we had expected*

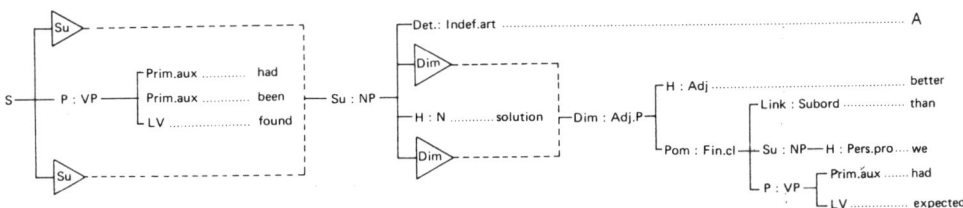

Sentence (6) is a simple sentence.

Sentence pattern: Su—P—Su

Note that this sentence contains a discontinuous subject (*A better solution . . . than we had expected*) which is realized by a noun phrase that contains a discontinuous modifier (*better . . . than we had expected*).

(7) *The policeman called my wife a doctor*

This is a simple sentence, which is two-ways ambiguous and consequently has two different analyses (a third interpretation, viz *The policeman called my wife, who is a doctor*, is only possible with a pause between *my wife* and *a doctor*, indicated in writing by a comma):

(a) Su–P–DO–OA (meaning: 'The policeman said that my wife was a doctor').
(b) Su–P–BO–DO (meaning: 'The policeman called a doctor for my wife').

We will only provide a tree-diagram for analysis (a):

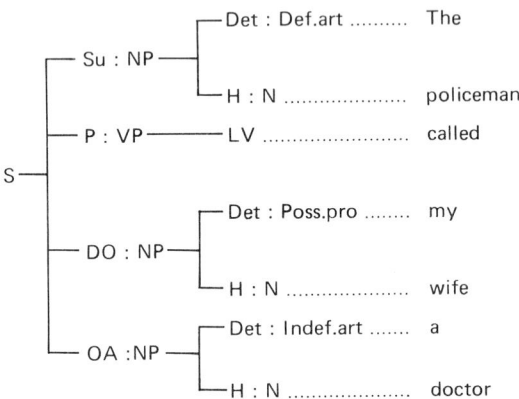

Sentence (7) is a simple sentence.
Sentence pattern: Su–P–DO–OA.

The following are examples of the analysis of complex and compound sentences.

(8) *I remember Peter saying that he had refused to join the party*

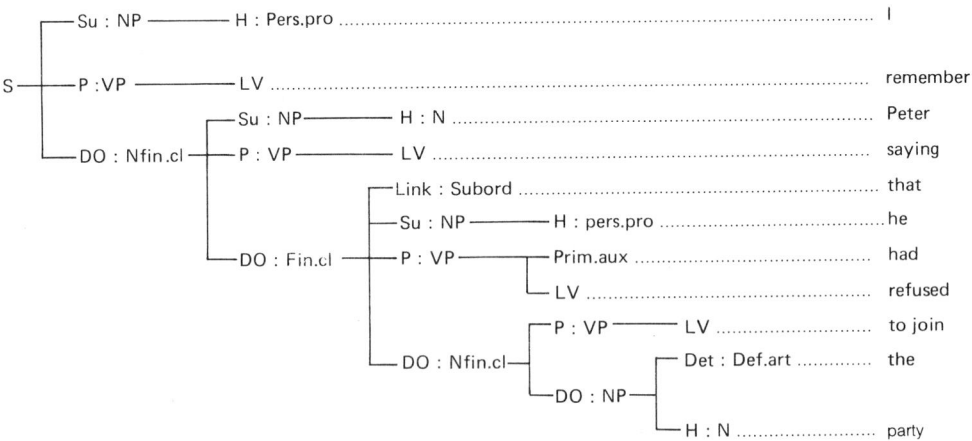

Sentence (8) is a complex sentence, since the function DO is realized by a (non-finite) clause (*Peter saying that he had refused to join the party*). Note that this clause contains a DO clause (*that he had refused to join the party*) which, in turn, contains another DO clause (*to join the party*).
Sentence pattern: Su–P–DO.

(9) *Would you mind being called a liberal?*

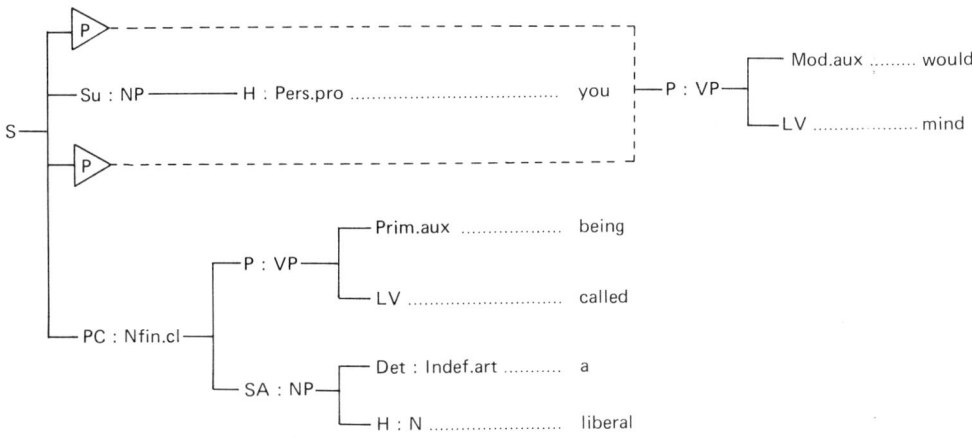

Sentence (9) is a complex sentence, since the function PC is realized by a (non-finite) clause (*being called a liberal*).

Sentence pattern: P – Su – P – PC

(10) *Our students have discovered that it is possible to enjoy grammar*

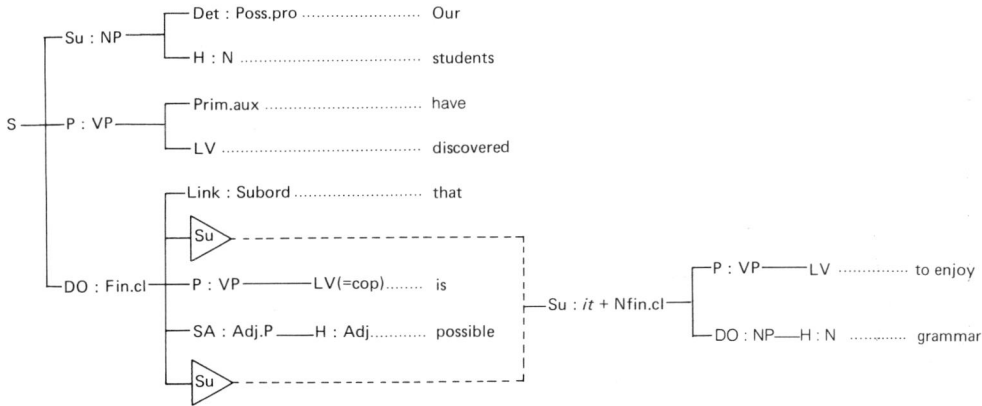

Sentence (10) is a complex sentence, since the function DO is realized by a (finite) clause (*that it is possible to enjoy grammar*). Note that this clause contains a discontinuous subject (*it + to enjoy grammar*).
Sentence pattern: Su–P–DO

(11) *We found it very hard to find a suitable candidate*

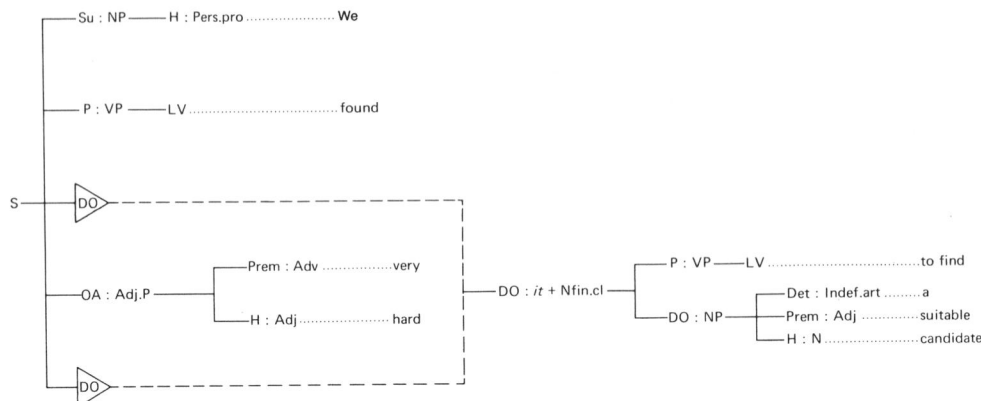

Sentence (11) is a complex sentence, since the function DO is realized by the (discontinuous) sequence *it* + non-finite clause (*to find a suitable candidate*).

Sentence pattern: Su——P——DO>——OA——<DO

(12) *I have never known David do irresponsible things*

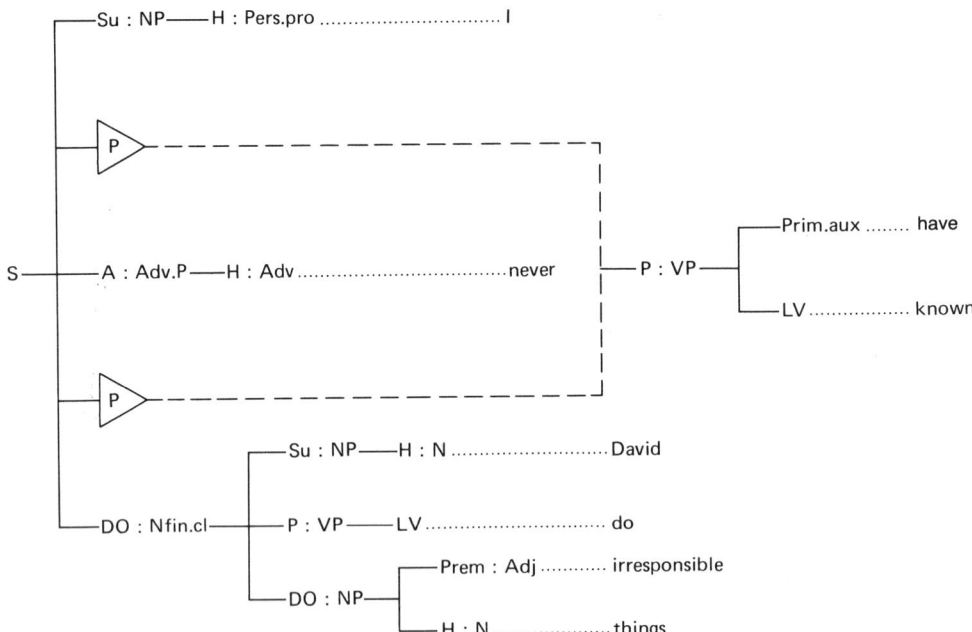

Sentence (12) is a complex sentence, since the function DO is realized by a (non-finite) clause (*David do irresponsible things*).

Sentence pattern: Su——P>——A——<P——DO

(13) *Freddy left early because he had promised to take Joan to London*

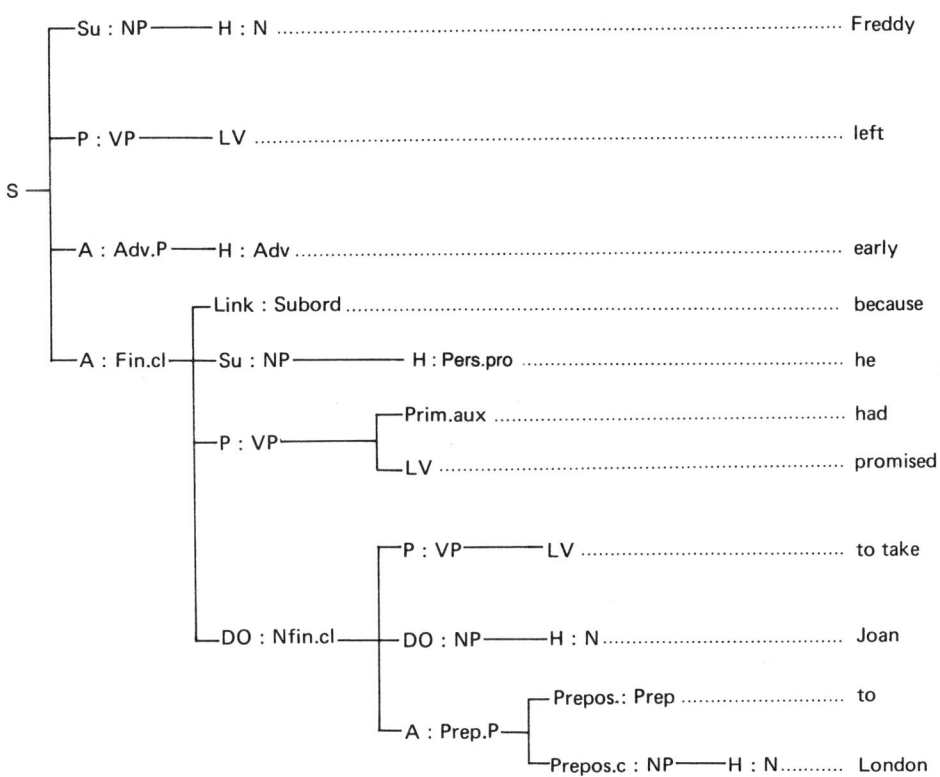

Sentence (13) is a complex sentence, since the second function A is realized by a (finite) clause (*because he had promised to take Joan to London*). Note that the function DO in that clause is realized by a non-finite clause (*to take Joan to London*).
Sentence pattern: Su–P–A–A.

(14) *Though very ill, Oscar finished his autobiography in the summer*

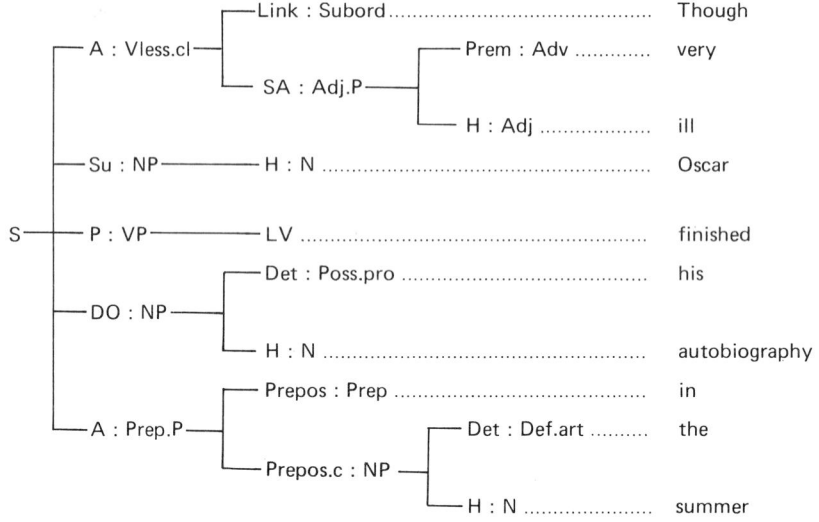

Sentence (14) is a complex sentence, since the first function A is realized by a (verbless) clause.
Sentence pattern: A–Su–P–DO–A.

(15) *Jane supports Frank but she is wrong*

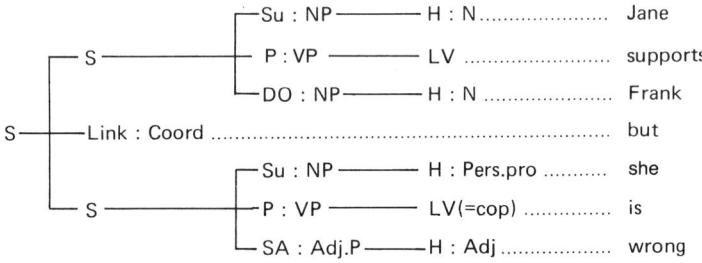

Sentence (15) is a compound sentence, since it involves coordination. The two conjoins are simple sentences: *Jane supports Frank* (Sentence pattern: Su–P–DO) and *she is wrong* (Sentence pattern: Su–P–SA).

(16) *I think that Barbara is a doctor but Ruth says that she works in a*
      library

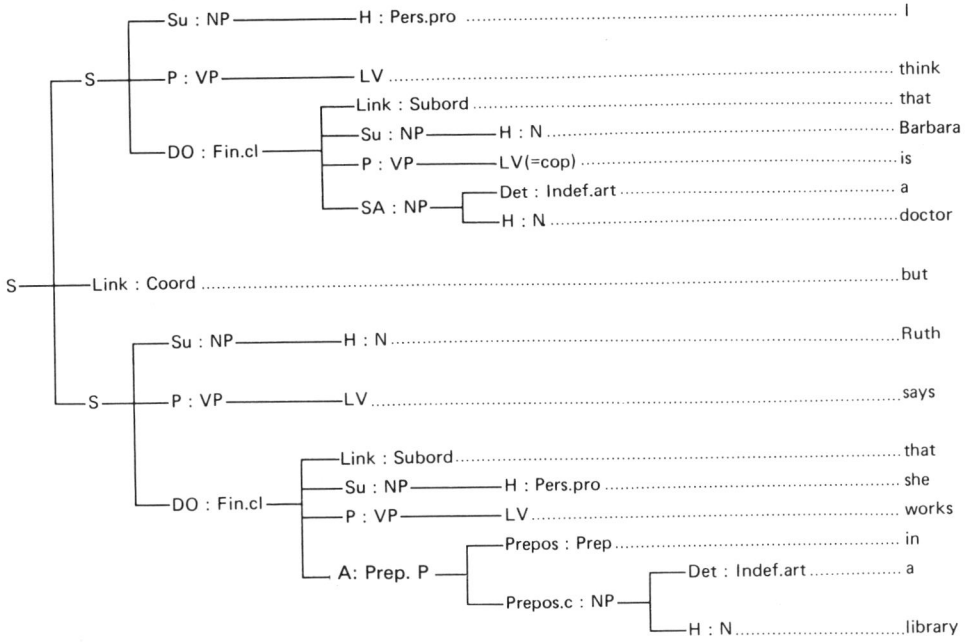

Sentence (16) is a compound sentence, since it involves coordination.
Both conjoins are complex sentences and both belong to the sentence pattern Su–P–DO.

List of abbreviations

Functions:

A	: Adverbial
BO	: Benefactive object
Det	: Determiner
Dim	: Discontinuous modifier
DO	: Direct object
H	: Head
IO	: Indirect object
Link	: Linker
OA	: Object attribute
P	: Predicator
PC	: Predicator complement
Pom	: Postmodifier
Prem	: Premodifier
Prepos	: Prepositional
Prepos. c	: Prepositional complement
SA	: Subject attribute
Su	: Subject

Categories

Adj	: Adjective
Adj. P	: Adjective phrase
Adv	: Adverb
Adv. P	: Adverb phrase
C. num	: Cardinal number
Coord	: Coordinator
Cop	: Copula
Def. art	: Definite article
Dem. pro	: Demonstrative pronoun
Ex. *there*	: Existential *there*
Fin. cl	: Finite clause
Indef. art	: Indefinite article
Int. pro	: Interrogative pronoun
LV	: Lexical verb
Mod. aux	: Modal auxiliary
N	: Noun
Nfin. cl	: Non-finite clause
NP	: Noun phrase
O. num	: Ordinal number
Pers. pro	: Personal pronoun
Poss. pro	: Possessive pronoun
Prep	: Preposition
Prep. P	: Prepositional phrase
Prim. aux	: Primary auxiliary
Quant	: Quantifier
Rec. pro	: Reciprocal pronoun
Rel. pro	: Relative pronoun
S	: Sentence
Self-pro	: Self-pronoun
Subord	: Subordinator
Vless cl	: Verbless clause
VP	: Verb phrase

Index